Claude of France
THE STORY OF DEBUSSY

Claude of France

THE STORY OF DEBUSSY

By Harry B. Harvey

ILLUSTRATED BY SALCIA BAHNC

ALLEN, TOWNE & HEATH, INC. · NEW YORK

The author dedicates this story to those who have, in one way or another, helped to develop his appreciation of Claude Debussy's life and music:

JOHN ALDEN CARPENTER

GEORGE COPELAND

GEORGES DUTHUIT

MARY EVARTS

DOROTHY HARVEY

EMMA HOYT

AND

MAGGIE TEYTE

ACKNOWLEDGMENTS

GRATEFUL ACKNOWLEDGMENT is made to the following for permission to quote selected material from their biographies of Debussy:

Dodd, Mead and Company for *Debussy: Man and Artist* by Oscar Thompson. Copyright, 1937, by Dodd, Mead and Company.

Oxford University Press for *Claude Debussy* by Léon Vallas, 1933.

E. P. Dutton and Co., Inc. for *Debussy* by Edward Lockspeiser, 1936.

The author is also indebted to the writers of two French books from which he has taken the liberty of translating several paragraphs: André Suarès' *Debussy* and René Peter's *Claude Debussy*. These writers are credited wherever quoted.

I

1

"*Our little one will be chosen, I am sure.*"

FROM THE WINDOW on the fourth floor of an old French house on the rue Pigalle, a small boy leaned out, anxiously watching the courtyard below. Surely, he said to himself, the postman *must* come soon! Then the concierge would look over the letters—perhaps among them could be the one he had watched for on many silver October mornings.

This was the Paris of 1873, and the eleven-year-old child was Achille-Claude Debussy. Pale and not too robust-looking, his eyes dark under his mass of black hair, his face was sometimes somber, sometimes lighted up with sudden interest. In this house he had lived with his family, and here he had been working for three

[3]

years with the hope of being accepted as a piano student by the famous Conservatoire of Paris.

Down in the court he saw the concierge interrupt her vigorous sloshing of water over the stones to pull the *cordon* in response to a knock at the big outer door. The postman stepped through the smaller entrance, and Achille could hear his polite exchange with the concierge. She turned and looked up, waving a letter.

"It is for you, Monsieur," she called, adding the title in honor of one receiving so official-looking an envelope.

Little Achille, his eyes now glowing with excitement, rushed out into the hall, and fairly tumbled down the worn stone stairs. He could not wait for the concierge to pant slowly up the four flights. Already breathless, but smiling sympathetically, she met him at the second floor.

"*Voilà, mon petit.* I hope it is good news."

She waited, thinking to hear more, but Achille only stammered "*Merci, Madame,*" and hurried upstairs to find his mother. Together they read the longed-for news, which told them that Achille would be allowed to compete, and was to present himself at the Conservatoire on the following Tuesday morning!

Only three days away—what a flurry of preparation in the Debussy home, what excitement among his two brothers and his sister Adèle! The least nervous was the young musician himself, who watched with calm interest while his mother mended and brushed his best little suit. Of course he could not, for this great occasion, wear the customary black sateen blouse and leather belt of the Paris schoolboy.

Tuesday morning they set off, Achille and his mother, accompanied by his devoted teacher, Madame Mauté de Fleurville, for the old building in the Faubourg Poissonnière.

The competitions were held in a large grim hall, before an impressive jury presided over by the director, Ambroise Thomas. His special privilege was to frown alarmingly at the frightened applicants to be sure they realized the honor and importance of the coming trial. (Thomas is remembered today as the composer of *Mignon,* an opera frequently given in America, and the less-known *Hamlet,* heard occasionally in Europe.)

At the end of that long day of hopes and disappointments, an official took his place solemnly in front of the waiting assemblage of candidates and their anxious parents, demanding their attention with a preliminary cough.

He began to read the names of the winners of the coveted honor, and it was pitiful to see some of the faces, old and young, as they listened for those that might never be heard. There had been sacrifices made by these parents—were they to be in vain? Madame Mauté, sitting beside Victorine Debussy, patted her shoulder reassuringly.

"Our little one will be chosen, I am sure," she said.

Their suspense was mercifully brief. In a very few moments the reader of the list announced: "Achille-Claude Debussy."

Achille, who had been sitting in unbroken silence, sprang up and threw himself into his mother's arms. Then he was engulfed in another ardent embrace from Madame Mauté. She beamed with pride; here was her reward for years of untiring patience.

Naturally there must be a celebration. They departed for their favorite chocolate shop, where they were joined by Achille's father, loud and hearty in his expressions of joy. He had doubted the wisdom of planning a musical career for his first-born; it seemed an unpractical choice, since a musician seldom earned a good living. Now his misgivings were gone. Was not Achille enrolled in the great Conservatoire of Paris! In another ten or eleven years he would emerge, an eminent pianist well able to help support the family!

Manuel-Achille Debussy, the father, had never done well as a provider. Up to the time of his marriage he had tried several jobs without success, the last one as an accountant for a Paris firm. He soon tired of columns and figures and, deciding to become a merchant, he took over a china shop in Saint-Germain, near Paris; there he went with his bride Victorine to live over the shop.

In that small house, 38 rue au Pain, on August 22, 1862, their first child was born. Not until nearly two years later was he baptized—in the family tradition—as Achille-Claude Debussy. His parents called him Achille—a name he considered "quite ridiculous" when he grew up, dropping it in favor of Claude Debussy. He kept a certain feeling of pride and affection for his birthplace; years later he said to an interviewer:

"Some think of me as a man of the North, a melancholy type. Others that I am from the South, from Provence—Daudet, tireli, tirela. . . . Well, I'm just a native of Saint-Germain, half an hour from Paris."

In the early years of their married life the growing family had a tough time of it, scraping and contriving. Their situation would have been worse but for the help of Achille's aunt, his father's sister, Madame Roustan, his own godmother. Not only was she kind-hearted, but she had rich and benevolent friends, and through them became a true benefactor, above all to Achille.

His father, having failed to prosper with the china shop, gave up Saint-Germain, moved to Clichy, and finally returned to Paris. He was lucky enough to find a steady job with modest pay, and settled on the rue Pigalle. His responsibilities had increased with a daughter and two more sons. Thus surrounded, and now partly supporting his family, he felt himself entitled to the French term of honor, *bon père de famille*. In time, however, Victorine Debussy was glad to accept Madame Roustan's offer to assume the care of all her children except Achille.

The *bon père* had no heritage of deep musical understanding to bestow on his son. He liked the lighter forms of comic opera and the melodious early works of Verdi. Once he took his son to a performance of *Il Trovatore,* which seems to have impressed the small boy. But there was never much companionship between father and son. Achille's natural perception led him to a greater sympathy with his mother, and he soon grew to appreciate her simplicity and devotion.

His mother could give him love, but she was baffled by the ways in which he seemed different from other small boys of the quarter. He had received little regular schooling, and Victorine had to do her best to teach him elementary lessons. But she had little education herself, and she failed to stimulate her son. He spent hours alone in his room, until his mother called loudly:

"Achille, where are you? You must come now for your lessons. What are you doing?"

"Nothing, *maman.*" Dutifully he dragged himself away from his small activities.

"Nothing! How on earth will you ever amount to anything? . . . Good, let us begin here."

It would have been useless to try to tell his mother he had just been "thinking." Or busy with the butterfly collection that fascinated him. Or cutting out pictures to pin on his walls—reproductions of paintings. Indeed, he even considered becoming a painter.

In all, Achille was a shy, unsocial little boy, lost in his own special thoughts, with small interest in other boys and their games. One exception was a devoted friend, who was to become a boon companion of later student days and throughout his life—young Gabriel Pierné, who was also to become a composer. Pierné gives us this picture of the youthful Achille when somewhat older:

"I remember very well how he used to delight in a cup of chocolate my mother invited him to take at the Café Prévost; and how, at a pâtisserie he used to choose a delicate pastry from a case specially reserved, while his friends were likely to be content with something more substantial.

"My father had a bound set of illustrated magazines. When Achille came to the house we used to look at the pictures with delight. One day he persuaded me to help him cut out these pictures to put on our walls. The crime was soon committed, and I remember he went off with reproductions of famous paintings, by Meissonier in particular."

This Achille Debussy, who lived within himself, was in striking contrast with the young bohemian, Claude Debussy, who in later years was to be delighted with hours of talk, wit and argument in his favorite cafés, usually lasting until early morning.

When he was seven years old, his mother received a letter from his aunt, Madame Roustan, which filled her with delight.

"But listen, my little one," she cried enthusiastically, "here is wonderful news for you. Your aunt is most kind. Wait, let me read you what she says: 'I am going to Cannes, for my vacation, as always. It would give me great pleasure if Achille and his sister could go along with me.' Isn't that splendid for you? To see that beautiful Riviera, and the Mediterranean! I've never been able to, myself, so I am all the happier for you."

She paused. Though she saw no eager response on her son's face, secretly he was pleased with the invitation. He may have been feeling already the emotion that the sea was always to evoke in him. At last he said:

"If you wish, *maman,* I shall be pleased to go with Madame my aunt. When do we leave?"

In Cannes the young Debussy found new vistas for his eyes, brilliant in the luminous air. Here was color—the amazing blue of sea and sky, the white, pink, and orange villas, the bright green of tropical palms and the darker verdure of the umbrella pines. And

in the sheltered harbor, the hundreds of masts and sails softly out-
lined against azure turning to rose at twilight appealed to his alert
sensitivity.

Claude Debussy, the man, had little to say of his boyhood
years, except for this period on the Côte d'Azur. In a letter written
in 1908 he recalled the road to Antibes, lined with roses: "I have
never seen so many all together in my life . . . the best way to
decorate a street." And he remembered a Norwegian carpenter who
"sang from morning to night; perhaps the songs were Grieg's."

His aunt encouraged him to make the most of the sunny climate
so different from Paris winter weather, with skies always ready to
weep. But she was practical as well as kind, and one day she had an
inspiration. For some time she had felt that Achille might have
undeveloped instincts for music.

"Listen, Achille," she said, "how would you like to take piano
lessons?"

"Piano lessons, dear Aunt?" echoed the little boy.

"Yes. Begin to study the piano. Why not? It seems to me that this
might interest you. I know of an Italian teacher named Cerutti who
lives near by, and I'm told that he has both ability and patience.
Wouldn't you like him to give you lessons?"

So it was from the elderly Cerutti that Achille-Claude Debussy
had his first instruction in music. His teacher discovered no special
signs of talent, certainly no evidence of the genius his pupil was to
demonstrate later. The lessons were just a task undertaken by
Achille to please his aunt, to show appreciation of her kindness.
But they must have taken hold of him, for when he went back to
Paris he found diversion on a worn-out piano that somehow had a
place in his home. In his odd fashion, he liked to "play" on it, to
make up chords, and try to imitate music he heard on the streets.
The habit soon became the means of revealing his gifts to the one
who really started Achille Debussy on his musical career.

2

"I will give him lessons with the greatest pleasure."

On the Place Pigalle, very near the Debussy home, stood a merry-go-round, a *carrousel*. Late into the night the gaily painted horses whirled endlessly, urged on by the strident blaring of a mechanical organ. One afternoon, forgetting that he was bringing cakes home for a guest his mother expected at teatime, eight-year-old Achille lingered, fascinated by the scene. Not by the music, certainly; his attention was all for the wooden steeds and their elaborately dressed riders. Something about the shifting colors appealed to his pictorial sense; the entire neighborhood, with circuses and carnivals coming and going, had a special charm for this silent, solemn child. At last he moved away, looking over his shoulder, his mind now on the cakes he carried.

Entering the family parlor, overfull of furniture and ornaments, Achille paused shyly at the door. A strange lady was sitting there with his parents.

"At last, here is that bad boy, always late," his mother exclaimed. "Now we can have our cakes. Madame, this is my son, Achille-Claude. Say good evening, my little one, to Madame Mauté de Fleurville. She is a renowned musician."

"But, no, Madame," the lady replied quickly. "That is too great a compliment. Say rather, a serious student."

"But you have studied with no less than the great Chopin himself!" Victorine had recently heard this, though she had only the vaguest idea who Chopin might be.

Achille's dark eyes opened a little. He, at least, knew about Chopin. But he offered no comment beyond saying politely, *"Bonsoir, Madame."* He had little curiosity about strangers, and was mutely begging permission to be excused from a social occasion that failed to interest him.

"Here, Achille, I will give you two little cakes and a cup of tea. . . . Now run along to your room."

Her son, with a jerky bow, gladly took himself off to his pictures, his butterflies, and his old piano.

"But he has a most interesting face, your little boy," Madame Mauté observed. "So intelligent. That is why I have come to call on you," she went on to explain. "My son, Charles de Sivry—he composes music—met your boy on the street the other day and talked to him. Charles told me he thinks that Achille perhaps has a talent for music. Have you yourself ever noticed any signs of this?" she asked, turning to the boy's father.

It had never occurred to Manuel-Achille Debussy that any of his children might be gifted—or even intelligent; but now he made a show of paternal pride.

"Oh, yes—he has studied the piano a little. His aunt, Madame Roustan, was good enough to arrange for lessons when he visited her at Cannes. With an Italian, Cerutti. But I fear—"

"Truly?" interrupted Madame Mauté, all alert. "But Cerutti is *good!* A trifle old-fashioned, but sound. I would like to hear your son play."

"That, alas, would not be easy to arrange," Victorine sighed. "He doesn't like to play before people. I wish he were different."

Back in his room, the subject of their conversation had completely forgotten the presence of the guest in the parlor. From examining his pictures one by one, he had passed on to his butterflies, and then to the piano. Here he began his own special style of strumming, always incomprehensible to his father and mother.

The acute musical ear of Madame Mauté was instantly engaged. "But listen. He *is* playing something. . . . Yet I do not recognize—"

"That is the trouble," Monsieur Debussy broke in. "He is like that. No melody of the kind *I* enjoy. No *tune!* Now you take Verdi—"

Having no wish to "take Verdi," Madame Mauté interrupted; for an idea that had come to her must be launched immediately. "My friends, your Achille *has* talent—genuine talent; and what is more, an originality that is astonishing. I can hear this, even in the way he is playing now. He must become a musician, a pianist," she persisted firmly. "And I should enjoy giving him lessons—without charge, naturally. What do you say?" She looked from one to the other.

Achille's parents, overcome by such generosity, protested politely, but to no effect. Madame Mauté de Fleurville continued to insist, and finally they gave in, still wondering, but highly gratified. Their son's artistic development was to begin.

That Achille never forgot her patience and wisdom is shown in a letter he wrote his publisher, Durand, over forty years later: "To Madame Mauté de Fleurville I owe the little I know about the piano." She was gifted with the ability to convey to her pupil what she had learned, and to encourage him to work hard. She could arouse his interest in the artistic life of Paris, in the personages of the most cultivated society, which she knew intimately.

Yet during the three years that Achille was her pupil neither of them had any thought of his becoming a composer. He worked only at piano-playing, and—unlike many other great musicians when young—felt then no desire to write down creative fancies. How different from Franz Schubert, who began as a child to pull scraps of ruled paper from his pocket and scribble snatches of melody that haunted his mind!

It was not until six years had passed that the young Debussy began experiments in composition. He was fourteen when he first wrote out any music of his own.

These had been the significant events in Achille Debussy's life, before the day of his admission to the Conservatoire. We have described the happiness of Madame Mauté, who had made his achievement possible. Let us see how his new life began, from his first entrance on the stage of work and progress.

3

"*Why must there be rules? I hate rules.*"

T HE PALE SUNSHINE sifted through the dusty windows of a small, cluttered room of the Paris Conservatoire. It was hardly more than a cell, but it lay apart from the active corridors of the school and offered privacy to its occupant, Albert Lavignac, instructor in *solfège*. He was only too glad to have these remote quarters assigned to him as the youngest member of the faculty.

Sheet music and scores spilled off the two tables and from the top of the upright piano in the corner. Tilted back in a chair, his feet on another, M. Lavignac was not applying himself to the students' exercises spread out on the table before him. On the contrary, he was entirely at ease and carefree. The young professor—he was only twenty-six—was enjoying a last cigarette before the long, hard routine of his day of teaching.

Unlike other instructors at the school, who were old in years and experience and pedantic by nature, M. Lavignac was always eager to detect early signs of talent in the entrants of the season just beginning. The rest of the teaching staff, devoted to rigid rules and formulas, felt slight interest in discovering latent gifts among their students. In being assigned to this sympathetic young master for his first work in the Conservatoire, Achille was far luckier than he could realize.

There was a faint tap on the panel. Lavignac called out in a welcoming voice: *"Entrez donc!"*

The door was pushed open on ancient, reluctant hinges, and before the master stood a short, thick-set figure. Lavignac could see at once that the boy was embarrassed, and said quickly and pleasantly: "Good morning, my little one. Have the goodness to enter and put yourself at your ease. What is your name?"

Reassured by his friendly reception the child came slowly into the room.

"Good morning, Master," he said with hesitation. "My name is Achille-Claude Debussy. They tell me that I am to be in your class."

"But that is very good. I shall be enchanted to have you. Do sit down," he said, waving to a chair.

He had not happened to hear about this candidate. As he had not been present at the entrance trials the name meant nothing to him. It was merely Lavignac's nature to be polite and encouraging to every new student. He looked closely at Achille as the boy moved awkwardly to the indicated chair and perched himself on its edge, waiting for Lavignac to speak again. He pulled off an odd cap with a red button—a souvenir he cherished from his days at Cannes. It was the kind worn by sailors then, and is still worn by the boys of the French navy.

Here was a pale and none too healthy-looking lad, aloof in manner, yet apparently ready with a certain shy response if encouraged. For the moment his eyes were devoid of any expression. Nevertheless, Lavignac was able to guess at an active intelligence when awakened by interest. The young Debussy's marked characteristic was the prominent forehead, often referred to during his life as his *double-front*. The instructor observed that his clothes were of the sort worn rather by children of the working class than by students at the Conservatoire.

Presently Lavignac found himself a little baffled by the continued silence of this strange boy, staring at him as if asking what next? Certainly the teacher had no gift of clairvoyance that might have told him he was in the presence of a future immortal. . . . At last he fell back on stock questions:

"Have you had training? Piano? The science of music—*solfège?* Tell me, please."

"Some piano, sir. In Cannes several years ago with a Signor Cerutti; and recently I have studied with Madame Mauté de Fleurville. But *solfège* . . . no, sir."

"Ah, Madame Mauté. She is admirable. You could have had no one better—especially for Chopin. And Cerutti—I think I have heard of him as a sound, conscientious teacher."

There was another long pause. Lavignac's curiosity about this odd specimen suddenly suggested an interesting detour from routine. He pointed to the piano in the corner.

"Play something for me, please. Anything you like; improvise in your own way, perhaps. Let it come out as you feel and pay no attention to the rules—don't even think about them!"

Such flouting of the most sacred traditions of the famous school would have shocked Lavignac's older colleagues. But he was rewarded by seeing Achille's somber eyes brighten. The little boy hoisted himself up on top of the scores that filled the chair in front of the piano.

With no conventional introduction he launched forth. As described later by Gabriel Pierné, "he used literally to throw himself on the keyboard and exaggerate his effects. He seemed to be in a rage with the instrument—ill-treating it with his impulsive gestures and breathing noisily as he performed the difficult passages."

Though Lavignac heard a series of astonishing chords that instantly aroused his attention, he sat without comment or protest while Achille piled up unexpected harmonies and complex rhythms that were new to the master, and doubly amazing from so young a student.

"Tiens!" he said to himself. "We're going to hear something from this little boy."

Abruptly, after a final dissonant and unresolved chord, at which other professors would have shouted in protest, Achille stopped and climbed down from the chair. Lavignac, politely responsive, concealed his excitement over this wonder. He began to speak slowly, carefully choosing his words:

"Very interesting. Very novel. Very—shall I say—courageous. . . . But, my little one, with me you must forget these explorations for a time. I am engaged by the Conservatoire to teach my pupils as well as I can the science of music—"

Feeling that the boy was about to interrupt him, he held up his hand, and went on determinedly:

"You must understand that in no other school is the course of *solfège* so rigorous. You must learn not only to sing at sight and transpose readily. I must also lead you to acquire the knowledge to analyze and reproduce any harmonic texture, before you can begin the necessary study of harmony with M. Durand."

Lavignac was pleased with this admirable speech, dictated by his conscience, though he doubted whether some of the big words had been really understood. Disregarding the mutinous look clearly visible in the dark eyes, he rose briskly. But the young Achille-Claude Debussy spoke up stoutly:

"Why must there be rules? I *hate* rules!"

"At the moment, my son, that is not for me to say. As you go on we shall perhaps find an answer. Certainly you must study *solfège*, hard and long. All pupils at the Conservatoire must."

"But why must I be like the other pupils?"

This outrageous speech was too much for even Lavignac's tolerance, although he had difficulty in smothering a laugh.

"Come," he said, and gestured invitingly to the little rebel. "It is time to go. I will now take you to my class in *solfège*."

4

"He doesn't like the piano, but he does like music."

IT was indeed well for the young Debussy's introduction to the
Conservatoire that he had made a friend of Lavignac. For
in the advanced piano class which he joined at once, he found
a far different situation. Here was an instructor of another kind;
and here was hostility at once from Achille's fellow pupils. His personality failed to please them and they showed it. Instead of help
and encouragement, he encountered constant repression, which before long became open antagonism.

The piano teacher was Marmontel, an old man who had been
teaching at the school for thirty years. He was tired of trying to
encourage the efforts of young students. Instead of mellowing

with age, Marmontel had only become more sarcastic and brittle.

"Here you are at last, my boy," was his standard remark to Achille on many a morning. The child had a habit of tardiness which the pedantic teacher found unbearable. Naturally the greeting brought snickers from the other boys, anxious to curry favor with the master. And Achille's odd clothes and silent manner deprived him of the easy popularity often earned by less gifted but more sociable boys.

With a muttered apology he would make his way clumsily to his place, and the work of the class was resumed. During many of Marmontel's dry lectures the other pupils noticed Achille's restlessness. He was bored and inattentive because he saw no sense in such methods of teaching. Above all, he disliked intensely the kind of technical piano exercises he was forced to work over.

"He will never learn to play the piano, that one," a malicious pupil whispered behind his hand to his neighbor.

"No—he *is* a queer sort!" was the reply.

As time went on that first winter, Marmontel became daily more irritated by poor Achille. One day he discovered that his pupil was spending his own study time poring over the scores of great composers, instead of preparing his exercises for the next day's class.

"What is this? *What is this?*" the master stormed, his voice growing shrill. "How do you expect ever to become a pianist? Such things are not for a little boy like you. . . . Get back to your regular work, I tell you—at once!"

With no answer except a weary sigh, Achille closed the book before him and turned to the exercises.

One day as he was passing quietly along a corridor, from around a corner he heard his name mentioned. He stopped where he was, without being seen. Marmontel and another teacher were enjoying an exchange of complaints about their students.

"This young Debussy now," he heard Marmontel say, "I find him very difficult. He doesn't like the piano, but he does like music."

Achille turned and made his way back along the hall. He was both injured and infuriated by what he considered another injustice from old Marmontel.

"It simply isn't true, what he says," he muttered to himself. "Of course I am fond of music—and I'm fond of the piano too. But what could anybody learn from that old idiot?"

For all his customary diffidence, Achille grew bolder when he was aroused by the kind of comment he had overheard. So the next day, when his teacher called on him to play a standard piano piece, he took an impish pleasure in further exasperating Marmontel: he introduced shocking innovations into the classic, supplying a daring prelude and some involved interludes. And how delighted he was by the violent reaction he evoked! Marmontel shouted angrily at such liberties, and called upon the class to demand whether they had ever heard such nonsense.

To them, naturally, such a performance seemed just as shocking. Like Marmontel, they could hardly realize that they were witnessing the first growing pains of genius. But the curiosity of one of the more intelligent boys was aroused; he must have guessed that there was more in this rebellion than appeared on the surface. During study hour a little later he came upon Achille engaged in his secret perusal of scores. He went over and sat down by the explorer in forbidden lands.

"Tell me, Achille, which of the great composers interests you most?"

"This, for one," Debussy answered, indicating the score of a Mozart string quartet that lay before him.

"And what is it you are making there?" the boy inquired, pointing at some illegible jottings on a sheet of music paper.

"I am working on a piano arrangement of this quartet," Achille answered proudly and confidently.

His friend was astonished and a little awed. What daring for a first-year piano student—arranging Mozart! Impertinence, even . . . Yet he could not help being impressed and asked Achille who were his other favorites.

"Most of all, Johann Sebastian Bach, even if he is sometimes long-winded. Also Haydn . . . and Schumann . . . and Chopin, about whom I learned much from my former piano teacher, Madame Mauté"—with a touch of youthful pompousness. "She knew him well."

The questioner, more and more astonished at his fellow student's wanderings from the academic course of piano study, sat without speaking until Achille stirred uneasily—time was being wasted; at last he said politely but firmly: "Now, my dear friend, if you'll excuse me I would like to get on with my work."

He turned back to his Mozart, at once forgetting all about his interviewer, who wandered away, shaking his head in perplexity. Such goings-on in the Conservatoire de Paris!

Meanwhile in Lavignac's class the instructor worked hard over his interesting pupil, showing no public partiality and subjecting him to the most severe routine in all details of *solfège*. Achille in his turn repaid these efforts by also working hard to comprehend rules, and even grew more tolerant of restrictions under Lavignac's guidance.

Before many months the class routine was not enough to satisfy the special interests of either student or master. Both of them sought outlets for wider understanding. The teacher was fascinated by his pupil's musical sensibility, and gave him much of his own free time after the regular hours of the school. He was determined to teach Achille how to know and appreciate the music of the masters. Together, in solitary evenings after the Conservatoire had closed and everyone was gone, they spent hours under a single light in the darkness of the old building. They would go over the scores of old and new works, and late at night they had to make their way out through darkened halls.

It was on one of these evenings that Achille-Claude Debussy had his introduction to the works of Richard Wagner, a composer he was first to worship, and then much later repudiate with scorn.

"Here, Achille," Lavignac said on that memorable evening, "is the overture to *Tannhäuser*. Let us try to play it. It is extraordinary, colossal! You might be interested to know that when this opera was first performed in Paris the audience hissed. Well, we've learned better since. For Wagner is without doubt the greatest genius in modern music."

As they went through the four-hand arrangement of the overture, Achille kept crying out in astonishment, overcome by this new music. "But this is magnificent, Master!" he would exclaim. Or again, "See now, how here the key changes." When they finished Achille was ecstatic; he had had a glimpse of unknown heights. He fell into deep thought for a few moments and then turned to Lavignac with a triumphant expression on his face:

"Certainly, Master, the great Wagner doesn't trouble himself over rules!"

During his first year at the Conservatoire, though his progress at the piano was not perceptible and he had constant difficulty with Marmontel, Achille's real development came through Lavignac. To him, more than to any other instructor at that time, must be given a place of honor, for it was Lavignac's quick intelligence that was the first to perceive that here was no ordinary music student. Nor was the boy's development due only to Lavignac's insistence on hard study; his rapid progress sprang still more from the private sessions with the master. The benefit was not all on Achille's side, either; Lavignac owed to his protégé's sharp questions a definite quickening of his own ideas, a gradual but sure change in his views. Often he had to admit to himself that he really agreed with some of the boy's heretical notions!

But he never relaxed his discipline in the "rules" that Achille so often proclaimed his hatred of. For Lavignac was a good teacher, and as such could not fail to make plain to the boy, over and over again, that the hated rules were really the essential basis on which the art of music had been built, and that—however passionately Achille wished to break away from them—he must first be thoroughly familiar with them, so as to know *why* he was defying them. Lavignac reminded him that the Mozart and the Schubert whose music he adored had been grounded early in the traditional principles before they were ready to start out on fresh paths of their own.

Altogether, the friendship between the instructor of twenty-six and the boy of eleven proved a fruitful one, and the team a winning team. At the end of the first year, in 1874, Achille had become so proficient in what he considered the boring "science of music" (for how could any art be also a science?) that he won the third medal in *solfège*. For a newcomer in a large class it was a real achievement at his age.

Which was all very fine, but in his piano work the picture was different. His continual disputes with Marmontel were creating an atmosphere of disapproval among the rest of the faculty. "What indeed," they were asking, "is to be done with a pupil who flouts all the rules, and who remains unimpressed by the scholarship of his teachers—and quite indifferent to the serious study of the piano?"

The day approached for the first performance of the advanced piano class—a public competition among the pupils. It was a day of trial and anxiety for all the young aspirants. In the inclosed world of the Conservatoire, public competition was all that counted; no other method of examination meant anything. On the important day, therefore, pupils, relatives, and devoted friends gathered in the old concert hall, gazing respectfully at the august faculty prepared to sit in judgment.

Achille-Claude Debussy's first public piano performance, in July 1874, was of Chopin's Concerto in F minor—a work that makes great demands on any pianist, especially on a boy not yet twelve years old. By this time the black sateen blouse had been discarded forever, since Achille had learned a thing or two from his young associates, and now he came to the platform dressed in a neat, double-breasted suit, with a broad white collar spreading over the lapels of his coat. Madame Debussy and Madame Mauté looked at him with fond pride.

The next day at home the verdict was complacently received by his mother, but it came as a surprise to Achille, who remembered Marmontel's continued disapproval. Flanked on either side by his eager parents, the budding artist read his first press notices, and learned that he had received second honorable mention!

Enthusiasm mounted high in the Debussy apartment when in one newspaper the family read that "This little boy of eleven exhibited a degree of confidence and vigor that are remarkable in a child of his age." But depression followed quickly when they turned to a less indulgent reviewer: "The youngest pupil is not yet twelve years old; he obtained the second honorable mention because to youth much must be forgiven."

"An imbecile, no less!" raged Manuel-Achille Debussy. "An imbecile, this pig who writes so contemptibly about my son."

On this note of conflicting opinion ended Achille's first year at the Conservatoire de Paris.

5

"It is all utterly unorthodox, but still, it is very ingenious."

"WHAT MADNESS! What desecration!" stormed the director-in-chief of the Conservatoire. "How can anybody like you ever hope to become a truly educated pianist?" This was Ambroise Thomas, who had presided at Achille's entrance test and had ever since been increasingly irritated by him. He was another of the older men of the faculty who were prejudiced and intolerant about any new ideas among the students. Thomas lived entirely in another world and day of music, and everything about this upstart only served to exasperate his conservatism.

When the pupils appeared before him on examination days, he nodded in benign approval of the careful performances by the well-disciplined boys. But on this occasion, Achille, playing from Bach's *Well-Tempered Clavier,* had not been able to resist introducing some of his own innovations, and had brought down a torrent of heavy sarcasm.

In the fall of Achille's second year at the Conservatoire, he continued to be a storm center. Nevertheless it was a year of progress in his studies, and in 1875 his anxious father's hopes took a leap forward, for his son captured the first honorable mention at the public piano competition and also rewarded Lavignac's devotion by winning the second medal in *solfège.*

At the piano competition Achille played Chopin's second *Ballade,* and this time there were no adverse criticisms in the Paris papers. They called him "a child who promises to become a remarkable pianist" and "a boy of twelve destined to be a first-class virtuoso."

"First-class virtuoso." The phrase fell pleasantly on the paternal ear of Manuel-Achille Debussy.

"Now, Achille," Lavignac told his favorite pupil, "in spite of this depressing October day I must tell you that you are now to begin work in a new field of music—and under not the best conditions, if I may speak thus about a man much older than myself."

It was the autumn of 1876; at the age of fourteen Achille Debussy had begun his fourth year at the Conservatoire.

"It is time to start on the study of harmony," Lavignac went on, "and for that there is only Durand. He, I may tell you confidentially, has no interest in his profession, little in music, and least of all in pupils mistakenly intrusted to him. It is your bad luck, but what can be done? It is like Marmontel again, only worse."

Lavignac had found in the silent Achille an outlet for his own rebellion against the dull faculty of the Conservatoire; he knew Achille would never quote him. In Emile Durand he saw an instructor with neither imagination nor inspiration; the type of second-rate teacher who was more likely to reach high position than a man of originality and real ability. This dried-up character was appalled by the liberties his pupil took with his harmonic exercises. Durand was even more shocked than Marmontel or Thomas had been. There are many stories of these conflicts, and years later one of Debussy's fellow pupils recorded his own impressions of what a genius had to contend with during the early years of his education.

The lad was one Antoine Banès. He described the way in which Durand, after dutifully marking the exercises of the other boys, would pounce upon Achille's work like a child who has saved his greatest treat for dessert. Sarcastic comments crackled in the close air of the classroom, while his savage pencil stabbed unmercifully at the sheet before him, defacing the paper with heavy black marks.

Banès, just the same, noticed that the professor of harmony, having vented his first rancor, always began a second and silent reading of the exercise he had practically destroyed. Something compelling about these exercises, as the months went by, forced him to yield a little to the influence of the dominating young student. Toward the end of that year he was heard to say to himself, scrutinizing the sheet before him:

"Of course, it is utterly unorthodox, but still, it is very, very *ingenious.*"

During that very year, and from this uninspiring soil, sprang Debussy's first known composition—a song called *Nuit d'étoiles,* to words by Théodore de Banville, now seldom heard. The poet was a follower of Victor Hugo and Alfred de Musset, but was also called a precursor of the "Symbolists," a new school of French poets.

At the end of the previous season his father had looked forward to the third piano competition. But, alas, the parental barometer was to fall swiftly. Achille was required to play the first movement of Beethoven's great sonata, Opus III. The selection was a complete misfit for his abilities and for his taste, although he had worked hard on it. At this time he thought he "abhorred Beethoven," so he was out of sympathy with his assignment.

The glowing prophecies by the critics of 1875 flickered out. No prize was given to him, nor was he even mentioned in the press. It was a bitter blow to Achille's pride, and the good papa was again in deep mourning.

Achille sought distraction by a brief period of studying the organ with César Franck, but soon left this by-path to devote himself more assiduously to the piano. Still urged on by his father, he was not ready to give up the idea of becoming a piano virtuoso.

He advanced in mastery of the instrument, so much so that in 1877 he sent his father's hopes rocketing upwards again—by sharing the second prize with another pupil for his playing of a Schumann sonata. Also he won the first medal in *solfège*. Monsieur Debussy was able to gladden his eyes with this glowing tribute from the *Journal de Musique:*

"M. de Bussy, for whom last year we predicted a brilliant future, is fulfilling the promise of his previous performances. He is only in his fourteenth year. In his fifteenth year, M. Marmontel's young pupil will surely carry off the first prize."

Achille's father embraced the boy ardently. "See, my son," he exulted. "For just a year or so longer you'll have to work hard, and then the real career of a virtuoso will be yours."

"But, Father—" The boy stopped. It was useless to confuse his father now with objections to a career in which he was no longer interested.

In 1878 came a sharp upset, an even crueler disappointment. Achille not only won no first prize, as had been so optimistically predicted, but received only scant and patronizing notices in the newspapers. "He has plenty of time to improve his style and technique, as he has not yet attained his sixteenth year," one critic said.

In a kindly moment Achille's father conceived the idea that a decided change of scene might benefit his son and soften his disappointment.

"Listen, Achille, here is something you might do now. Friends of mine are to go in August to spend a few days in London. I am sure they would be happy to have you go with them; you are old enough now to see more of the world."

The suggestion suited Achille perfectly. He had a natural craving for travel, and he left Paris for the Channel steamer in high spirits. He felt that he had put childhood behind him, and was well on the way to becoming a young man. And it was suitable for a young man to know something of London.

In the great metropolis Achille enjoyed the sights and sounds with a youth's eagerness, and the most lively impression he brought back was a performance of the Gilbert and Sullivan operetta *H.M.S. Pinafore*, though the typically British humor and the unfamiliar type of music proved somewhat bewildering to his young French ears.

In the fall Achille returned to Marmontel's piano class without enthusiasm. He found it harder and harder to rouse himself to serious preparation for the competition in the following summer. He could not apply himself.

"How much longer do I have to stand this endless and stupid piano study?" he asked himself passionately.

As it turned out, not very "much longer." At the 1879 competition he played Chopin's *Allegro de Concert*—and his name failed completely to appear among the prize winners! One journal observed sardonically that he "seemed to be progressing backwards."

Such a failure, unquestionably the young pupil's own fault, was the final blow to Achille's father. It finished forever any hopes that his son might become an important—and profitable—figure in the world of eminent pianists.

"But, Father, I truly dream of being a composer. There are some who think I have gifts," Achille tried to say. "Lavignac now—"

"Pah, a composer—what is that?" the elder Debussy interrupted violently. "You cannot hope to become a great one. Here you have been in Durand's harmony class for two years now, and haven't won a single honor. And without honors you cannot even enter a composition class!"

This was unfortunately true. While the judges had had to acknowledge some charming ingenuity in his exercises, his disregard of old-fashioned rules had made it impossible for them to give him any prizes.

"So then what?" the indignant parent continued. "Do you expect to support yourself by starving in a garret? Ridiculous!" He stalked from the room, thereby sparing his son the need of making a reply.

Deep in his heart Achille was sure that he had within him the promise of greater achievements, and he was ready to relinquish with no regret a professional piano career. He was only seventeen, but his intelligence was maturing, and he realized that the six years he had spent in piano study without any practical result brought a deep disappointment to his father.

It was not that Achille had failed to become a really good pianist, for he had not. Later he was to find many uses for his piano technique, not only as an aid to composition, but also in making money in small ways. But he knew that he would never be able to make use of his pianism for conventional solo concert work.

Thus the year 1880 saw the end of Debussy the piano virtuoso. Yet it was none too promising for Debussy the composer. He went on with Durand's harmony classes, though with lagging interest. These past few years, however, had produced a handful of actual compositions. In 1876, for example, there was a song called *Nuit d'étoiles,* now deservedly forgotten; and in 1878 he completed another—*Fleur des blés.* These two are rarely revived, but a third song, *Beau soir,* proved to be of more lasting merit. The words were by Paul Bourget, another of Achille's favorite poets during his early years. All three have been called "mere drawing-room pieces," showing the influence of Massenet, who dominated many composers in the late '70s. But *Beau soir* still appears often on recital programs because of its fluid, lyrical charm.

Before Achille had found a practicable way to begin real work on the study of composition, his stay in Paris was unexpectedly interrupted by one of the most stimulating episodes of his boyhood.

6

Interlude à la Russe

DURING THE SUMMER VACATION of 1880, M. Marmontel, by this time more tolerant of the rebellious youth who had so often annoyed him, summoned Achille to his office at the Conservatoire.

"Now, Monsieur Debussy," he began, paying ironic tribute to Achille's eighteen years, "here is an almost unbelievable opportunity for one of your tender age. It should transport you with delight. I have here a letter from none other than Madame Nadejda von Meck."

The professor of advanced piano, now well over sixty, had to fumble for his spectacles in order to read the fine script on the elegant thin paper. First he explained:

[33]

"Madame von Meck, you must understand, is very, very rich, a Russian aristocrat in every sense. She is a widow with eleven children, though now only fifty. Imagine! She is a fine pianist and a renowned patron of music and musicians. She loves ensemble playing with her friends and her children. From this letter it appears that she wants me to recommend a promising piano student who will join her household at Chenonceaux—they are living in France at present—to give lessons to her children and play piano duets with her.

"For this honor and privilege I have decided to propose you, my young friend. I do so with confidence, in spite of—shall I say—your regrettable deficiencies in my course. You have plenty of facility, and you do well at sight-reading. . . . In short, I urge you to accept this signal privilege. You will learn much."

Achille required no urging. He was immediately entranced by the picture of a pleasant summer of luxurious living in the castle of this "very, very rich" *grande dame*. He appreciated, too, the opportunity offered in such a musical household to advance his own knowledge and experience.

"But I must tell you, very confidentially," Marmontel resumed, "that Madame von Meck is mad about Tchaikovsky. She contributes generously to his support, though by reason of some eccentricity in her character she refuses ever to meet him or talk to him. It is enough for her to insure his comfort and his leisure to compose without worrying over living expenses, and to send him affectionate and encouraging letters. I tell you this because you will undoubtedly be expected to play a good deal of Tchaikovsky's music, and you should know that to Madame von Meck his name is sacred."

At the castle of Chenonceaux, with its lovely formal gardens, its surrounding moats, and the river running below, Achille found himself in a veritable musician's paradise. Music—expert, scholarly music—went on from morning until late at night. The shopkeeper's son became a member of the family and shared the comforts and luxuries made possible by a large staff of servants. He was assigned, among other duties, the piano part in the household trio of violin, 'cello, and piano that his patroness maintained at all times.

Madame von Meck could hardly be called beautiful, nor was she endowed with the mysterious fascination attributed to Russian ladies at the height of the Czarist regime. But she had nobility of character, and the dignity that belongs to the high priestess of a cult—her worship of Tchaikovsky. To Achille she was gracious, informal, and sympathetic—and at once understood her "little Frenchman," as she called him. In July she wrote to the Russian composer:

"This young man plays well, his technique is brilliant, but he lacks any personal expression. He is yet young, says he is twenty but looks sixteen."

Later she wrote again to Tchaikovsky:

"Yesterday I played for the first time our symphony * with 'Bussy'. . . . My partner did not play it well, though he reads at sight splendidly. That is his only, though very important, merit. He reads a score, even yours, like an open book. . . .

"He does not care for the Germans, and says 'they are not of our temperament; they are too heavy, not clear and light.' On the whole he is a typical product of the Parisian boulevards, . . . very witty and an excellent mimic."

How happy would have been our "man" of eighteen to hear himself thus described! For even in the warm, friendly life made by Madame von Meck and her family, he still lacked assurance. He

---

* Madame von Meck and Tchaikovsky always called his Fourth in F minor "our symphony."

was often ill at ease and clumsy, except when encouraged to express some of his unorthodox ideas about music and traditional teaching.

In September Madame von Meck took her entire household to Italy, where Achille went right on with his absorbing musical life and immersed his senses in the beauties of Florence. At the Villa Oppenheim there, he worked out several small compositions, including his first piano piece, a *Danse bohémienne,* which his patroness sent to Tchaikovsky for comment.

"A very nice little thing," the master wrote, "but altogether too short. Not a single thought is developed to the end, the form is bungled, and there is no unity."

In Florence, Achille had his first love affair. Although he was constantly with Madame von Meck's daughter Julia, as her regular accompanist for songs, it was her younger sister Sophie he decided to honor with an offer of marriage. The charming Sophie was only sixteen, and Madame von Meck promptly and firmly declined. There was no more of that, and the young man suffered no permanent injury. But it was not to be long before he embarked on a really ardent attachment.

That summer the family traveled to Venice, and on to Vienna, then one of the great capitals of the music world—all to the delight of the travel-loving "little Frenchman." In Vienna he heard for the first time *Tristan und Isolde,* conducted by the greatest of all Wagnerian directors, Hans Richter. What emotions the young pilgrim felt as the climaxes of the music-drama piled up, one after the other, almost beyond his endurance! The impression that *Tristan* produced on Debussy was one he never quite forgot, even when much later he repudiated Wagner as a genius.

It was Achille's magic summer of new music, new scenes, new experiences. Most gratefully he appreciated the vistas that had opened before him through his intimate association with this gifted family. Among other tokens of gratitude he produced a trio for the household ensemble.

"Imagine," Madame von Meck wrote to Tchaikovsky, "that boy cried bitterly when he left. Naturally I was deeply touched. . . . He would not have gone at all if the Conservatoire had not refused to prolong his leave."

The following year Achille begged Madame von Meck to let him return to her musical court. She agreed graciously, and in July 1881 he joined his patroness in Moscow. Here, through the days and long evenings, the intense musical life, the worship of Tchaikovsky, the songs, piano duets, and trios went on with the same energy as before. Achille was in Heaven again!

At nineteen, the young Debussy began to regard himself as quite the man of the world, and found new distraction in the society of Vladimir von Meck, the eldest son. He was a frivolous young man, popular in Moscow society, and he at once supplied the diversions that had begun to interest Achille. Together they went to the Moscow cabarets, and "Bussik"—his nickname had become Russianized—was wildly enthusiastic about the gypsy music played and sung in these night spots.

Achille never saw his delightful friends again after the Russian sojourn. For two summers their way of life—their continual round of playing and singing—had provided an extraordinary new experience for his sensitive mind. He had dwelt in a musician's dream of Paradise—and at the same time been able to supplement the Conservatoire routine with "fruitful musical revelations of the highest interest."

Because he loved the von Mecks, Achille felt the utmost gratitude for the advantages they had given him. This he might well do; coming between youth and manhood, they left impressions of lasting value on his future.

Before his first summer with the von Mecks, in 1880, Achille had been favored by a stroke of luck that made it certain he could study to be a composer. Denied entrance to the course in serious composition by his failures to pass M. Durand's requirements, he had somehow managed to get admitted to the new score-reading course recently offered by August Bazille. Like Lavignac, Bazille recognized originality and was inclined to encourage it. His class in practical unwritten harmony suited Debussy exactly; he too had always been irritated by the theoretical study of harmony.

The tasks that this teacher imposed were difficult. But Debussy, "who felt at ease with the conscientious and broad-minded Bazille, soon reached the stage . . . where he excelled in solving the musical enigma of the given melody. . . . Bazille did not always approve of the modulations in which his pupil indulged. But just as Marmontel had realized the spontaneity of Debussy's talent, so Bazille also listened, growled, stormed, but ultimately gave in."

Bazille also believed that only at the piano could compositions be worked out properly. This had been Achille's own idea, and he was glad to soothe the stings of conscience over his failures at piano competition. Was he not to be a composer? Very well, then, he had learned enough of the piano to use it for composition—a method he was to favor throughout his life.

At this point the muses who preside over genius took charge of Achille-Claude Debussy. He won the first prize in Bazille's class! On the strength of his accomplishment other rules were waived, and he was allowed to begin the serious study of composition.

II

7

"These songs which she alone has made live."

UNDER THE HARD LIGHT that blazed over the billiard table of the Café-Restaurant de la Reine, the younger of the two players had just executed a very neat carom shot and won the game. The older said:

"Well, my friend, shall we have one more of these games at which you seem to beat me every time? Or better, perhaps, one more bock and a final cigarette at the little bistro on your corner, while we discuss our respective theories of music?" It was in this lively and unprofessorial manner that Ernest Guiraud, newly appointed instructor in composition at the Conservatoire, was in the habit of talking to Achille.

This Guiraud, although forty-three years old, was young in spirit. Like Lavignac and Bazille he could detect a young man's future possibilities. He believed Achille would develop faster if given extracurricular attention. Fortunately, Guiraud was a true *noctambule*—one of those birds of the night whom Debussy came to prefer to all others as companions. They had the same tastes: for billiards, cigarettes, much talk of music, aesthetics and painting. Guiraud was determined not to suppress his pupil's natural explorations in the entire field of art by too strict an observance of the usual teacher-pupil relations. Hour after hour into the night argument would crackle and flame, while all the time they became better friends, and the young student's range of vision widened under the influence of Guiraud's intelligence.

Guiraud had been a friend of Bizet and had known Berlioz; he had written several operas; he was a hard, serious worker. Like all composers of this period—in fact, as Madame von Meck had said of Debussy himself—he had been strongly influenced by Massenet. And as with Lavignac, Achille's friendship with him went far to neutralize the depressing effect of such teachers as Marmontel and Durand. He was liberal, adventurous, and the best of company, and the awakening intellect of his protégé could ask for nothing better.

At the Conservatoire, however, Achille was still regarded as a dangerous nuisance by the conservative members of the staff. Réty, the registrar, was quite unable to understand Guiraud's partiality for this rebel, and took every chance to express his old-fashioned indignation. One night he came by chance into a room where Achille was playing some of his incredible improvisations. Réty stopped the clamor with an imperious gesture.

"Do you imagine," he demanded shrilly, "that dissonant chords do not have to be resolved? What rule, may I inquire, do you follow?"

To which the youth made the famous answer that has become a classic:

"My own pleasure!" he said boldly.

The registrar could only walk out of the room, aghast at such insolence.

It was our troublesome young man's delight to pursue similar shock methods with the more timid pupils at the Conservatoire. "Attention, now!" he announced on a certain evening when there were a number of students assembled in a classroom. "I will show you on this piano how the buses sound outside on the Faubourg Poissonnière."

Then from the instrument came a strange chromatic groaning which only evoked derision from the listeners. He whirled around on the piano stool and surveyed the group mockingly.

"Look at them. . . . Can't you listen to chords without knowing their names? *Listen*—and if you can't understand it, go and tell the Director I am ruining your ears!"

The amazed auditors were then favored with a series of chords in combinations altogether incomprehensible to them, but which Achille insisted were "a feast for the ear."

He carried on these demonstrations not only in Guiraud's class, but in that of Léo Délibes,* whose music, though then in vogue, seemed "inadequate" to Debussy. It happened that on a Spring day in 1883 Délibes was away from his class. Boldly Achille proposed to take the master's place.

"Come," he announced, "I will feed the little orphaned birds." Taking advantage of their stupefaction he went on challengingly: "Dissonant chords must be resolved? Is that what you say? . . . Consecutive fifths and octaves are forbidden. Why? . . . Parallel

---

* Composer of the opera *Lakmé*, the *Coppelia* and *Sylvia* ballets, and many other works.

movement is condemned, and the sacrosanct contrary is beatified? For what reason, pray?"

Then he turned and attacked the piano as if he were angry with it, pouring out a series of wild arpeggios, triple trills in both hands, and other outrages on orthodox playing. This went on for an hour or more, in spite of jeers and protests, until one of the authorities came in and stopped the show that was being conducted by this "impossible fanatic."

It was in such an atmosphere of antagonism to his inner convictions, high-lighted by constant scenes that were almost brawls, that Achille-Claude Debussy stormed his way through the next three years at the Conservatoire. It was relieved only by the sustaining influence of Guiraud, who continued to believe in him and to direct his efforts toward the ultimate goal, the coveted *Prix de Rome*.

This honor, eagerly sought by all serious students of composition, offered the successful candidate three years of endowed residence and work at the Villa Medici in Rome, where he would presumably develop his gifts in material comfort. Achille had his doubts about how much he would like three prescribed years under further routine, yet hoped to benefit by the experience. After all, he could count on these years for adequate support, he reflected philosophically.

For he was old enough to be confronted with the need of actual support, his family being now of little help to him. He managed to pick up a couple of jobs, laborious, underpaid, and certainly beneath his abilities, but allowing him to indulge a little more freely in his favorite night life with Guiraud and other friends. He served as accompanist for a singing society conducted by Madame Moreau-Sainti; later he worked in the same way for the Concordia Choral Society of which the director was Charles Gounod.

The composer of *Faust* was in these years enjoying the peak of his fame, and made no secret of the fact that even then he regarded the young Debussy as a coming genius. He proved his interest in many ways, and when in 1884 the final decision on the *Prix de Rome* was to be made, Gounod's influence was powerful.

In the Moreau-Sainti class Achille met the young and beautiful Madame Vasnier—a meeting that initiated a new period in his life. Not only did her friendship and that of her husband help to mold his character; it stimulated him to greater musical effort, both in the Conservatoire and outside. For at once he fell violently in love in his youthful way with this wife of a much older man, a distinguished architect.

Achille's infatuation was regarded lightly and indulgently by M. Vasnier. His wife had a charming voice and adored music, and he himself was preoccupied with his profession. What danger in encouraging this presumably harmless youth, who could contribute so much to his wife's musical life? (It was, in a way, a preview of the situation in the composer's only opera, *Pelléas et Mélisande*.)

Thus began for Achille-Claude Debussy several enchanting years. M. Vasnier welcomed him to his home, sparing no pains to make him feel at ease there. In winter Achille got permission to study at their apartment on the rue de Constantinople; in summer he went every day to their country house at Ville d'Avray. As in the von Meck household, he found again a cultured atmosphere that delighted him, as well as the luxurious comfort not to be found in the modest Debussy ménage.

Debussy the pianist gave piano lessons to the Vasnier daughter, but Debussy the composer was far more interested in writing songs for Madame Vasnier. It is to this daughter, whom her teacher considered dull, that we owe a picture of Achille at nineteen:

"Debussy was a big beardless boy with clearly marked features and thick, black curly hair which he wore flat on his forehead. In the evening when his hair was untidy, suiting him much better, my parents said he was like a medieval Florentine. His eyes especially were striking. His personality made itself felt. His hands were strong and bony and his fingers square. . . .

"I can still see him in the little salon in our flat on the rue de Constantinople, where for five years he wrote most of his compositions. He used to come nearly every evening, leaving the music he wrote on a little table. He composed sometimes at the piano . . . and sometimes walking about."

In such surroundings Achille began to be disturbed by his own ignorance—he had had so little early education. He now read everything he could get hold of, including the encyclopedia, and eagerly accepted suggestions from the scholarly architect. Under Vasnier's influence he graduated from earlier favorites like Paul Bourget to the poems of Paul Verlaine and Stéphane Mallarmé.

His first important group of songs, written in 1880-3, however, included two poems by Bourget, *Voici que le printemps* and *Paysage sentimental,* and also his first Verlaine composition, the fascinating *Mandoline,* always one of the delights of singers who can manage its difficult intervals. Nor was it long before the combined spell of romance and music inspired Achille to create for Madame Vasnier four charming songs to words by Verlaine, Mallarmé, and de Banville.

At Ville d'Avray the young musician's life suited his every taste. After working with Mademoiselle at the piano, they varied the routine with walks in the neighboring park and with interminable croquet games. He was a good player, but—just as with the cards they sometimes played on rainy days—always a bad loser.

Achille was hardly to be counted on to make himself pleasant at the gatherings of the Vasniers' friends, though by adroit handling he could be put into a good humor. Sometimes he was not even polite to other guests who failed to take his fancy. He resented strangers for no apparent reason; but if they pleased him he could be vastly entertaining, playing Wagner scores and imitating or caricaturing modern composers. The Vasniers forgave their difficult visitor everything because he was charming when he wanted to be and because they could see his genius develop before their eyes. Achille did not lack appreciation of their generosity and tried in every way to show it, by entertaining their visitors and by lending his help at the family concerts.

At a fancy-dress ball he and Madame Vasnier sang a duet he had written for the occasion. It made an odd picture—the beautiful woman with her trained, lovely singing and the awkward youth half her age, with his strange husky voice. The benevolent architect beamed indulgently at the pair.

Vasnier either was unaware of Achille's adoration of his wife and of her interest in him, or chose to consider the situation of slight consequence. Achille himself had no misgivings, and succeeded in keeping up his friendship with them both for several years.

As a tribute to the first great love of his life he wrote this dedication in an album of his songs:

To Madame Vasnier

These songs which she alone has made live and which will lose their enchanting grace if they are never again to come from her singing fairy lips.

The eternally grateful author.

8

"Besides, I felt that I was no longer free."

DURING THE YEARS when Achille Debussy was wandering along romantic by-paths he was not neglecting his serious work at the Conservatoire. Guiraud would never have permitted this. "Perhaps," he told himself, "the young man derives benefit from these friends, who are truly musical. It lends variety to his life, and that should help his regular study. Within reason, though! He must work for this *Prix de Rome.*"

Guiraud's interest in his precocious pupil steadily increased. The instructor was broad-minded, but he warned Achille against going too far in his musical venturing at this time.

"Now for instance," he observed late one night at their favorite café, looking at a score the student had written for *Diane au Bois,* a poem by de Banville. "This music you have here is all very interesting, but you would do better to keep this sort of thing for later on, or you will never get the *Prix de Rome!*"

He was right and Achille knew it. In spite of the fact that the youth's head was now full of plans to organize a revolution against musical dogma, he was clever enough to realize that such ideas must be suppressed if he wanted to earn the award. It was hard for him to give up the malicious pleasure of annoying the faculty with "outrageous chords," but he resolutely kept them for Guiraud's private and unofficial ear. Under the guidance of this master he worked hard that winter to develop a style of composition that might come within academic restrictions.

For the *Prix de Rome* final competition of 1883, the students were required to make a setting in cantata form of Emile Moreau's poem, *Le Gladiateur*.

The contest in July was a brilliant event, with Charles Gounod as the presiding judge. All the newspapers spoke in high praise of the competing works and their manner of presentation. Achille, with one of his fellow students, played his score at the piano, with the services of three eminent singers. His strongest competitor was his friend Paul Vidal, who had also been a piano pupil with Marmontel.

When the performances were finished, after a long, solemn conference the judges announced their decision. Vidal was given the first prize and Debussy the second! Achille's consolation was that the critics called it a very close contest—one of them insisting that there should have been two first prizes. "While M. Debussy was less expert than M. Vidal, he had more originality."

After the demonstrations were over, the two comrades went to the home of Achille's parents for celebration, of which Ernest Guiraud took charge with tact and good spirits.

"Come, Achille, it was a very close contest," he said cheerfully,

[49]

raising his glass of wine. "After all, you are younger than this Paul. Next year, now . . ."

Next year? Would there be a next year for him, thought the second-prize winner. In spite of public praise and private congratulation, he was deeply discouraged over failing to win the first prize, and next day he told the Vasniers that he had a mind to give up the struggle. What was the use? He wanted nothing more of the Conservatoire. He would turn his back on its dreary routine and its old walls.

Argument with the stubborn young man went on late into the summer night at Ville d'Avray. At last he allowed his sympathetic friends to prevail: he would go back in the fall and work hard and seriously for one more trial.

Unquestionably he did toil faithfully during that year when he became a man in the full legal sense. Constantly advised by Guiraud, he turned away from musical rebellion and sought the smoother path that might lead him to triumph in the summer of 1884.

Not only through Guiraud's expert knowledge, but also by exposing himself to outside influences, Achille tried to increase his understanding of contemporary composers. He had a great enthusiasm for Edouard Lalo, and attended performances of his works with devotion. And Massenet! In January and February he listened to performances of the operas *Manon* and *Hérodiade* and acclaimed them revelations in operatic beauty.

"Of course," he observed to M. Vasnier on one occasion, "studying the music of contemporaries under such conditions is very pleasant. But that Conservatoire! I would find it hard to go on there except for my friend Guiraud—and for Monsieur Gounod. Every week I see him at the meeting of the Concordia Society. Afterwards, over a glass of wine, he talks to me with such wisdom, such graciousness!"

That last winter of 1884 at the old school, Debussy had so many amusing and lively evenings with Guiraud and others, so many excursions to opera and concert, that the year could hardly be called a dreary grind. At the Conservatoire he conformed to the rules, and wasted little time disturbing the complacent peace of masters and pupils.

To honest labor—and genius—will ultimately come the fruits of success. On June 27, 1884, before he had passed his twenty-second year, Achille-Claude Debussy won the *Premier Grand Prix de Rome,* with almost unstinted critical praise. One review was prophetic:

"M. de Bussy, the hero of the competition, is a musician who is destined to meet with a great deal of praise . . . and plenty of abuse! At any rate, he is the most *alive* of the candidates this year and for many years past. The very first bars of his score reveal a courageous nature and an outstanding personality."

The poem chosen for this final competition was *L'Enfant prodigue* (The Prodigal Son) by Edouard Guinand. For the vocal parts the composer was fortunate enough to have the same eminent baritone, Taskin, of the year before, the great soprano Rose Caron, and one of the finest of tenors, Ernest van Dyck of Belgium. The orchestral score was played on the piano by Debussy and his friend René Chanserel.

It was a marked event in Paris musical life and almost a clean sweep for the winner of the *Grand Prix.* His cantata, written in twenty-eight days, had melodic and dramatic qualities notable at this period, with certain effects often used by Massenet. Debussy acknowledged it himself—it was a touch of strategy likely to influence the judges more favorably than his own characteristic innovations. The work was dedicated with deep gratitude to his master, Ernest Guiraud.

Out of twenty-eight judges, twenty-two voted for *L'Enfant prodigue*. During their long deliberations the composer had stalwart support from his loyal friend and admirer, Charles Gounod. Yet not all of the critics agreed with the verdict. There were mutterings; and several disgruntled writers insisted that the Debussy work was inferior to that of Charles René, one of his competitors.

Guiraud was elated, and felt well rewarded for the devotion he had bestowed on his gifted protégé. The Vasniers were equally delighted; Achille's parents were ecstatic. "I told you so," boasted the excellent papa—quite forgetting the gloomy picture he had drawn when his son renounced the piano in favor of a composer's career.

And what were the actual emotions of the "hero" of the competition? He had won the *Grand Prix!* But that meant leaving for an interminable period his beloved Paris, leaving the Vasniers and all his gay and congenial companions. Owing to the unselfish interest of those who wanted him to succeed, and to a certain obstinate pride in triumphing over his oppressors at the school, he had arrived. What for? What good was it? How would three years in the restricted surroundings of the Villa Medici help him to the musical independence he craved?

Many years later Claude Debussy recorded his own reactions on his "great day":

"I was on the Pont des Arts awaiting the result of the competition, and watching with delight the scurrying of the little Seine steamers. I was quite calm, having forgotten all emotion due to anything Roman, so seductive was the charm of the gay sunshine playing on the ripples, a charm which keeps all these delightful idlers, who are the envy of Europe, hour after hour on the bridges.

"Suddenly someone tapped me on the shoulder and said breath-lessly:

" 'You've won the prize!'

"Believe me or not, I can assure you that all my pleasure van-ished! I saw in a flash the boredom, the vexations inevitably incident to the slightest official recognition. . . . Besides, I felt that I was no longer free!"

III

9

"Here I am in this abominable villa."

W HEN THE PASSENGERS for Rome alighted from the Paris train at the Monte Rotonde station on a January evening in 1885, the weather was damp and forbidding. It was no better than Paris, thought the disgruntled winner of the *Prix de Rome,* turning up his coat collar against the rain. His spirits were as heavy as the elements. All the way down he had become more and more depressed, and from Marseilles sent a note to M. Vasnier, confessing his low state of mind.

He made his way along the platform until he was suddenly confronted by three young men who hailed him with joyful shouts of greeting. According to the time-honored custom at the Villa Medici, they had made the long trip from Rome to welcome their colleague to his new life.

"Behold our young hero, arrived at last!" one of them cried. Then from another: "How goes it, my little one? But wait—what has happened? Our friend now has a magnificent beard!"

The beard was hardly that, but it was black, and impressive enough for a young man of twenty-three. Its owner embraced his friends. *"Bon jour,* Paul! . . . Georges, you are looking well. And Gabriel, my dear friend. It is very good of you to meet me!"

These were Paul Vidal, with whom Debussy had competed in 1883, Georges Marty, and his lifelong friend Gabriel Pierné, earlier prize winners—now all studying at the Villa Medici. Achille did his best to show appreciation of their effort, but could not make it come from the heart. He thought his friends had changed; they seemed to have lost much of the good-hearted friendliness of their Paris days. "They're stiff—impressed with their own importance," he thought; "too much *Prix de Rome* about them."

All four spent an uncomfortable night in one small room and arrived the next evening at the beautiful Villa, the "Maison de France," which had been the property of the French government since 1803. Achille was installed in an enormous green room, nick-named the "Etruscan Tomb" by the students, with its massive furnishings long distances apart.

He saw himself as a desolate and lonely young man. Imagining hostility on the part of his former companions, he thought only of his discomfort in an alien atmosphere. . . . It was not a promising start for a young composer, condemned to spend three years in what he regarded as a prison.

Within a few days of his arrival, Achille poured out his general displeasure in a long letter to his friend, M. Vasnier.

"Here I am in this abominable Villa. I can tell you that my first impressions are not very favorable. It's awful weather—rainy and windy.

There was no need to come to Rome to get the same weather as in Paris, especially for anyone who has such a prejudice against Rome as I have.

"The first evening I played my cantata, which was very well received by some, but not by the musicians, I don't mind. This artistic atmosphere and *camaraderie* we are told about seem to me very exaggerated. With one or two exceptions, it is very difficult to talk to the people here, and when I hear their ordinary conversation I cannot help thinking of the fine talks we used to have together."

It is hard to understand how Debussy could have been unmoved by the beauty of the Villa Medici and the superb panorama he could see from its windows. He never found a good word to say even for the enchanting gardens on the slope of Monte Pincio, dating from the time of Napoleon.

Through pines, laurels, and statues he could see the dome of St. Peter's, a portion of the Leonine Wall, and the Castle of Sant' Angelo. It was a spectacle deserving ecstatic tribute, but it left the young Achille cold. He summed up the place, once and for all, as a "cosmopolitan hotel, a private college, and a compulsory military barracks."

When Achille arrived, the head "jailer" of his prison was M. Cabat, a painter and a man of some distinction. He was not supposed to have much to do with the students of music, painting, or writing who were pursuing their studies at government expense. Cabat went in for being a business executive—which failed to please any of the pupils, and especially Achille Debussy.

Luckily, he was replaced before long by M. Hébert, another painter, but also a musician of merit. His chief defect in Achille's eyes was his violent antipathy to Wagner, at a time when Debussy was at the height of his fever over the immortal Richard. Many an hour that he should have been devoting to his regular work was spent with other enthusiasts studying the score of *Tristan und Isolde*.

During these first months Achille was well aware that he must do something to justify his endowment. It was obligatory on each student to prepare a new composition and send it to Paris as evidence of progress. The *Envois de Rome,* these works were called. But he found himself constantly hampered by the lack of privacy at the Villa, by its pervading sociability. He was anxious about his music, worried because he was getting nowhere. He spent long fruitless hours gazing blindly out of his windows at the Eternal City.

At last he forced himself to try to begin work—without any important "idea," as his first attempt disclosed. For a text he chose a French adaptation of Heine's *Almanzor,* and called his effort *Zuleïma.* It did not satisfy him, and in June he wrote another letter to his friends in Paris in which he called the subject "old and fusty":

"These great silly verses, which are great only in their length, bore me, and my music would be stifled by them. Then there's another thing: I don't think I shall ever be able to put music into a strict mold. . . ."

With *Zuleïma* discarded, Achille cast about for something else that might perhaps get him on the right track. He remembered the fragmentary notes he had shown to Ernest Guiraud, who had advised him to "keep that sort of thing for later." Now, he thought, the time was "later," and he decided to take it up again.

It was a poem by Théodore de Banville, the poet he admired extravagantly in his early days, called *Diane au Bois.* He felt that the subject had "lightness" in comparison with *Zuleïma,* and would be more suited to his individual style. He completed only one scene, and even this failed to please him. . . .

Thus, by the end of his first season in Italy, Achille Debussy had not only been static as a composer, but had accomplished nothing that could be submitted with pride as an *Envoi de Rome!* What to do in his situation tormented the young man. Yet in spite of dissatisfaction with *Diane,* out of his frustration came the famous declaration of independence which the composer Debussy wrote during that month of June 1885:

"I am sure the *Institut* will not approve, for naturally it considers that the path it prescribes is the only right one. But it can't be helped. I am too fond of freedom and my own ideas. This is the only kind of music I can write. The question is whether I shall be capable of doing it? I can't say. *At any rate I shall do my best to satisfy a few people. I don't care what the rest think."*

Never through the thirty-four years of life that followed this arrogant proclamation did he ever compromise with his "own ideas."

That summer he received an invitation from a certain Count Primoli to be his guest at the Count's beautiful villa by the seaside at Fiumicino. Achille was offered a comfortable, carefree life, with every need satisfied, including that solitude which after the Villa Medici he craved so ardently. His meals were brought to him; he spent hours alone at composition, or wandering over the slopes of the lovely Italian countryside. He came to feel that at last he was working well.

His satisfaction did not last long. Once back at the Villa, resentment returned and he wrote a passionate letter to M. Vasnier, begging to be allowed to give up the whole thing. He insisted that the place was doing him no good, and he would be better off in Paris.

M. Vasnier answered promptly, pointing out with reasonable logic that Achille would have no way of making a living in Paris. In the face of this unanswerable argument, Achille could do nothing but stay in Rome and make the best of it.

In the time already spent at the Villa, Achille had at least not wasted his opportunities to hear music that he could not hear in Paris. One of his characteristic traits was an eager curiosity about compositions that were new to him. So he was happy to discover the church of S. Maria dell' Anima in an obscure side street, and liked what he called its purity of style, in contrast to more elaborate churches. There he listened to masses by Palestrina and Orlandus Lassus which fascinated him.

"That is the only church music for me," he wrote. "That of Gounod and company seems to come from some kind of hysterical mysticism, and has the effect of a sinister farce."

With Paul Vidal he went to the Teatro Apollo to hear *Lohengrin*, a rather mild refreshment for an ardent Wagnerite fanatically devoted to *Tristan*. At other times he enlarged his classical education by attending the first performance in Italy of Beethoven's Second Symphony; and heard the great pianist Sgambati play Beethoven's *Emperor* Concerto. By contrast he was much addicted to shows of the Punch-and-Judy sort; they appealed to his liking for fantasy and to the special sense of humor he was now developing.

Achille came to know Sgambati and spent a memorable evening in the society of Franz Liszt, who visited the pianist's house with his friend Cardinal von Hohenlohe, himself a distinguished amateur. It was the Cardinal's idea to honor the young French composer by asking Liszt and Sgambati to play Saint-Saëns' Variations for two pianos,* which the two great artists were glad to do as a compliment to French music.

Not only that, but Debussy had the greater honor of performing himself for this master pianist. With Paul Vidal he played Chabrier's *Valses romantiques*. . . . Achille never saw Liszt again, for this was the great Hungarian's last visit to Rome before he died the following year.

There were other meetings in Italy that had their points of interest for a young musician and offered welcome variations from the routine of the Villa Medici. Through a slight acquaintance with

* On a theme of Beethoven, Op. 35 (1874).

Leoncavallo, Achille was able to visit Milan and talk with Arrigo Boïto, that great librettist for other composers, but with only one considerable opera, *Mefistofele,* as his own achievement.

Boïto sent Debussy to Sant' Agata to see Verdi. The composer was fifty years older than Achille, with *Otello* his most recent accomplishment, and *Falstaff* yet to be written. Verdi received the pilgrim graciously in his garden, where he appeared more interested in his vegetables than in music, and avoided discussion of his contemporaries. But he gave the young man a good lunch, and then left him to go back to his work among the greens.

These episodes played a useful part in the general experience of a musician, but they were not advancing his *Envois de Rome.* Nor was he any better pleased with life at the Villa. Many a day he wandered out into the streets of Rome, intent on another of his interests—a passion for Japanese art. In the shops he was always buying these *objets-d'art,* which he could ill afford. He never entirely abandoned the Japanese influence, and it was the inspiration of some of his later music.

It was early in 1886 that Achille's dislike of the Villa Medici boiled over into a violent scene with M. Hébert. Always a good actor, he put on quite a show and threatened dire consequences if the master would not allow him to make a visit to Paris. His "act" had the desired effect, and in February he turned up without advance notice at the home of his dear friends, the Vasniers.

Though M. Vasnier disapproved of his insubordination, Achille was made reasonably welcome. He could gaze again on his enchantress, and for two months he recaptured some of the charm of his former life. But M. Vasnier, always a man of good sense and a stickler for integrity, persuaded Achille in April to drag himself back to the "abominable villa."

His absence was overlooked by M. Hébert and his wife, who could forgive what they considered the strange ways of the genius they began to recognize. Yet quite perversely Debussy did not appreciate their tolerance; he even described it as a "nuisance": "They wish to make things pleasanter for me, but actually they are making them more disagreeable. . . . In Paris I should probably like them very well; here they are nothing more than jailers."

The slow months of 1886 dragged along, and by October Achille had still produced nothing he deemed worth sending to Paris for his *Envoi*. Realizing that the Vasniers might be wearying of his complaints, he found a new correspondent. This was a stationer and bookseller he had met in Paris, one Emile Baron, whom he now selected as a sympathetic listener to "such things, feeling sure they will be understood."

He wrote to Baron about Rome in his most ruthless style. The letter indicates a new development in his character—as an acid commentator, a role in which he later became famous. The Debussy that he was to be, after his final return to Paris, began to emerge.

"You mentioned how much you wanted to go to a town where it is always spring.

"Well, don't come to Rome, because at present this town, reputed to be sunny, is like Moscow, all covered with snow, and freezing cold. The Romans can't understand it. The coats they wear are too short in any case, and they don't seem able to get used to proper overcoats. But the snow gives a very pretty color to the ruins. It shows up their severe contours and makes them look clean. They are a thousand times better than under that perpetual blue sky and in their usual pipeclay color. . . . There are long processions of priests . . . some of whom, dressed in black, are like curious black radishes, and others, in red, like roguish pimentos."

On an afternoon late in 1886, Achille Debussy, winner of the *Prix de Rome*, from whom so much had been expected, sat in his room, wondering what he was going to do about it all.

"These accursed *Envois!*" he exclaimed aloud. "I have sent nothing; I have written nothing fit to send. Yet something must be on the way—and soon!"

He unearthed the beginning of *Zuleïma,* the music set to "those great clumsy words." For want of something better, he thought, he would fix it up and get it off, even if it seemed to him too much like Verdi or Meyerbeer. He finished the first part only and sent it to the Academy of Fine Arts in Paris. It was a lame effort, and got no more approval than it deserved. Paul Vidal and Gabriel Pierné sent *Envois* that pleased the Academicians and gave them the chance to draw unfavorable comparisons:

"At present M. Debussy seems to be afflicted with a desire to write music that is bizarre, incomprehensible, and impossible to execute. . . . The Academy hopes that time and experience will bring salutary modifications to M. Debussy's ideas and compositions."

Embittered by the verdict, Debussy determined to try just once more to send an *Envoi* in 1887, and then—

In February of that year he delivered to the Academy a work for orchestra and "wordless" chorus, inspired by Botticelli's painting "Primavera," which he called *Printemps*. It was not intended, he said, to be a "descriptive spring," but rather a human one—"implying the gradual blossoming of the joy of living from miserable beginnings in Nature."

At a reception at the Villa he played the piece on the piano with his friend Savard, with fair success. In Paris it received slightly better comment than the *Zuleïma* of the year before, though not of a character to enhance his standing with the severe critics of the Academy. There they continued to hope for "something better from such a gifted musician as M. Debussy."

They waited in vain for any more actual *Envois de Rome*. In that very spring of 1887, after only two years at the Villa Medici,

Achille Debussy shook its classic soil from his shoes and went back to Paris—not to revisit his prison until twenty years later. Before he left he wrote to M. Vasnier that he would rather do twice as much work in Paris than "drag out this life here." He begged his friends not to be too hard on him; their friendship was all he had.

In spite of this plea the cherished friendship was not to last for very long after his return. Achille had changed, without realizing it. It is due to Mademoiselle Vasnier that there is a recorded epitaph on the end of his relations with the Vasnier family. She wrote that when he finally came back the former intimacy was no longer the same. "He had evolved and so had we. We had moved and made new acquaintances. . . . Then little by little, having made new acquaintances himself, he no longer came and we never saw him again."

One of the new acquaintances he made, although only a boy of eleven when Achille was twenty-five, was to become a friend of many years, and the author of one of the very few "personal" books about Debussy—a volume of anecdotes and sketches of his personality, with little mention of the composer. This boy was René Peter, who was taken by his parents "to a dinner at the home of the poet Vaucaire. Debussy then called himself Achille. . . . His Assyrian aspect, his tone of blackness, his emphatic speech, his mythological name, all scared me."

Achille Debussy, who had this mildly terrifying effect on a boy half his age, had reached the finale of his preparatory years. During them his character and thought had been molded by the interest of Madame von Meck, by the loyalty and support of the entire Vasnier family, and by his contacts with the several eminent musicians who had come into his life during the Italian "incarceration."

It was around this time that he decided to drop his earlier name of Achille in favor of Claude Debussy.

Now at this turning point of his life, let us interrupt his story with a brief historical chapter showing how Debussy's own France came into being. It has a bearing on the development of that civilization in which he was to belong—a world centering in Paris, with its blending tones of art, music and literature.

10

"Liberty, equality, fraternity."

FOR ALMOST A HUNDRED YEARS France had been violent in its
search for democracy. Three times the bell had tolled the
death knell of autocratic authority. And three times the
pendulum had swung back to a compromise between the new-won
liberties and the ruling order. Then, following the disastrous Franco-
Prussian war, while the young Debussy was working through his
third term at the Conservatoire, the Constitution of 1875 established the Third Republic.

The first grand upheaval had come in 1789, on the heels of our
own American Revolution—both inspired by the 18th-century lib-
erals, Rousseau, Voltaire, and Diderot among them. The French
cataclysm lasted less than a decade, something like discipline setting in with the Directorate. Toward the close of the century, the

young General Bonaparte blazed his way to military glory and became First Consul of the realm, with almost absolute power. And in December 1804, at Notre Dame in the presence of the Pope, he crowned himself Napoleon I, Emperor of France.

The period of Napoleon's glory and decline lasted for eleven years. After his banishment to St. Helena in 1815, three monarchs of the line successively ascended the ancestral throne. But, one after another, Louis XVIII, Charles X, and Louis Philippe overstepped their powers; and in 1848 the Second Republic came into being. It was a brief régime, swaying from Left to Right and back again. In the same year, with a swing to the Right, Louis Napoleon (Bonaparte's nephew) was elected president. Again, like his illustrious uncle, he proceeded to set up an imperial throne, in 1851 becoming Napoleon III.

The fifty years between the two Napoleons had seen the almost untrammeled growth of French genius in Stendhal, Balzac, Delacroix, Baudelaire, Flaubert, Victor Hugo, and other creative Olympians. The France to which Claude Debussy was to return from Rome in 1887 was all the more fruitful because of their great achievements. It was a rich harvest to which he and his contemporaries fell heir.

All through the luxurious years of Napoleon III's Second Empire, a sinister menace to France was being wrought by the iron hand of Bismarck, with the French emperor oblivious to the danger. Too late, and utterly unprepared, in 1870 he was forced—by a trick of Bismarck's—to declare war on Prussia. After three crushing defeats within a few weeks Napoleon surrendered and was taken prisoner. On September 4, 1870, the Second Empire fell, and Paris entered the famous period of siege during which the people ate their dogs and cats and even the animals at the Jardin des Plantes!

At Versailles in 1871, the Prussian king, William, was hailed as

German Emperor, with Germany a united empire. The improvised French government at Bordeaux capitulated, the siege of Paris was lifted—and France faced civil war in earnest. All through the feverish spring of 1871 the fighting across the barricades went on between parties and factions of citizens, each side calling the other assassins. For two months the radical "Commune" governed the city and influenced the entire country, while the conflict spread from street to street. Victory finally went to the champions of bourgeois law and order.

It was for these to choose a government. The majority favored a king and designated the Comte de Chambord, descendant of Henri IV. But he believed in the sovereignty of the people, and refused to be king. Thus, at length, arose the famous Third Republic, which with its constitution of 1875 ruled France until the Germans again took Paris in 1940.

These mighty upheavals of the mid-19th century took a momentous part in shaping the life of Claude Debussy. They deeply influenced the world of art that prevailed when he returned to live in Paris in 1887. At the time of his birth, his parents had no doubt shared the Emperor's faith: "The Empire, it is peace." But later in 1870 he must have heard the cannons firing from Montmartre. Many years afterward, in 1914, when the Germans again threatened Paris, he wrote: "I've never had a rifle in my hands. . . . My recollections of 1870 . . . prevent me from being very enthusiastic."

The French people have a genius for politics, and a genius for the arts, but the two kinds of genius are seldom found in one and the same man. They were found in Victor Hugo and Lamartine; but offsetting these were writers like Flaubert and Baudelaire who— though living in the midst of political violence—never deviated from devotion to their art. From these, Debussy was an artist in direct descent. Wars could come and go, the causes for which they were waged could be more glorious or less; but for such a man art alone was imperious. Today that long line of creative artists, leading to Debussy and the writers, painters, and musicians of his time, constitutes the glory of the 19th century in France. And in their turn they indisputably owed a debt for their free achievement to the men who had three times rallied to the *Marseillaise* and spilled their blood for liberty, equality, and fraternity.

IV

11

"Some left him, only to return and adore him."

CLAUDE DEBUSSY, free from his Roman "jail," stood at the door of the French world of art when it was reaching the height of its 19th-century glory. It was the year 1887; he was twenty-five, with his creative life before him. The next five years were to be as fruitful as the five years before had been barren.

The scene was perfectly set for a young man with revolutionary ideas. The painters, the writers, and a few of the musicians were bent on overturning ancient idols. The young had taken over, and were ready to run the show; the day would soon come when they would triumph as moderns, as inventors of new and completely French modes of expression.

It would have been natural for Claude to make friends easily among these ardent spirits. They might have compensated for his lack of companionship at the Villa Medici, at a time when their quick understanding was most needed. But shyness, partly imagined, stood in his way. He was inclined to excuse it then; and even years later he begged off from a distinguished gathering by saying: "As for me, you know—I am a bear."

Fortunately, two years later (1889-90) Debussy was drawn into closer contact with certain advanced young artists through the fabulous Exposition Universelle of Paris, which excited them with the exotic music and native art of far countries. Their fancy was delighted by singers, dancers, and orchestras from Africa, Arabia, and the Orient. Buffalo Bill's Wild West show came with its American Indian dances, minstrel troupes with their "cake walk." Almost the entire world of native music and tribal lore passed through Paris to stir the imagination.

Our young Debussy, now calling himself Claude instead of Achille, was an infatuated visitor to this World's Fair. Like many another he followed the craze for abandoning classic models and seeking inspiration in contemporary life. Indeed, Debussy's own excitement over the Javanese *gamelang* found expression in the string quartet he wrote later.

During this first year back in Paris, Claude had a sudden impulse to make a pilgrimage to Vienna to see Johannes Brahms, who was "quite aware that the French musical public considers me the most German of contemporary composers."

Having heard something of the Brahms disposition, Debussy made no attempt to arrange an engagement beforehand; he would merely present himself at the great man's door and hope for the best. The journey seemed destined to failure; on his arrival in Vienna he wrote to Brahms and had no reply for days on end. Desperate at last, he called at the Master's house, only to be put off by a servant. Fortunately, at the last minute, he met a French lady who had been a pupil of Brahms. She was sympathetic, and managed to arrange a meeting—an invitation to lunch with only Brahms and herself!

At first the Master was cross and showed it; during the entire meal he spoke only once:

"Are you the young Frenchman who has been pestering me with letters and door-knocking at my house?" Claude acknowledged that he was.

"Well, I will forgive you, but don't let it happen again."

By the end of the meal, made mellower by his favorite French champagne, Brahms unbent and talked a good deal about German and French music, with comparisons favorable to the former. Except for Bizet: "To embrace him I would go to the ends of the earth," he said, and boasted that he had heard *Carmen* twenty times. From that point things went better, and the next day Claude was invited by Brahms—more than twice his age—to have dinner with him and go afterwards to *Carmen* for his twenty-first performance!

Before he left Vienna there was a farewell meeting, when Debussy was welcomed with genuine affection. At parting he was favored with all wishes for success and a fatherly embrace. It was as if the conservative present were saying Godspeed to the bold and adventurous future.

The good wishes, alas, were no help in the obligation that confronted Claude on his return to Paris. As a laureate of the Villa Medici, he still owed to the Academy an *Envoi de Rome,* even if not written during his stay there.

At this time there was a considerable vogue for the English pre-Raphaelite school of painters and poets: Dante Gabriel Rossetti, Burne-Jones, and their disciples. In Italy Claude had read a French translation of Rossetti's *The Blessed Damozel* . . . she who, leaning out from "the gold bar of Heaven, had three lilies in her hand, and the stars in her hair were seven." The poem appealed to him and he decided to try it as text for the belated *Envoi*. Before getting down to work he went to London to consult the Rossetti heirs about the necessary permission and to arrange for an English publisher of the score. But no publisher would take it, and he returned to Paris with no hope of making money from England.

Now he must apply himself to his *Envoi* night and day. One of these evenings, toiling over his score, he was glad to look up and see that favorite friend from his childhood, Gabriel Pierné, standing in the doorway. Gabriel's greeting was gay:

"Come, my friend! It is cold here. Enough of work for tonight. We shall be the better for beer and conversation. Let us go to the Brasserie Pousset!"

"Very well," Claude responded, "let us by all means go out. I am finding this job very difficult." He rose and put on the wide cowboy hat he affected, and the two comrades set off through the wintry streets to the warmth of the café.

At twenty-five Claude no longer had the look of youth. He was heavy and slow of movement. His black beard and colorless face, the big forehead with overhanging hair, marked him wherever he went. Many of his intimates called him "The Black One." At any favorite rendezvous of young men of promise in the arts his biting witticisms were applauded. One of his companions described him as he was at the time:

"I can still see the keen, black, heavy-lidded eyes. . . . There was something feline about him . . . yet gypsy-like, something passionate, yet self-controlled. He spoke very little of himself, but criticized his confrères severely. Any remarks he made were highly intelligent, though he was always reticent and elusive."

Tonight they were greeted with shouts of welcome, urged to sit down and take part in violent arguments that raged late into the night. Everyone quarreled or loudly agreed until the owner of the café said it was time to close. Undaunted, the group transferred their forum to the wet sidewalks of the early Paris morning. Amid the rumbling of vegetable carts they could be heard proclaiming their bold ideas to the silent streets. "We do not wish to represent objects, but rather, their reflections—the impressions they produce on us. . . ."

With a measure of agreement reached, these rebels against old conventions were at last willing to call it a night. Singly or in pairs they would disperse down the narrow, winding streets, Claude often returning to the sheets of music paper to continue with the almost indecipherable notes that were to become *La Damoiselle élue* (The Blessed Damozel).

The work went on through part of the following year, before Claude was ready to offer his final *Envoi de Rome* to the Academy —*La Damoiselle élue,* a cantata for two solo female voices, women's chorus, and orchestra. It was received by that august body with the usual reservations: "The text is rather obscure, but the music he has fitted to it is not deficient in either poetry or charm." Though the press was more favorable in its comments, no public performance of this, Debussy's first large-scale composition, was scheduled until 1890. For this occasion Debussy expected that his earliest *Envoi* from Rome—*Printemps*—would also be included on the program; and when the judges objected to this the angry composer refused to compromise and the event was called off. *The Blessed Damozel* was not publicly produced until 1893, five years after he had completed it.

Notwithstanding such setbacks, the tide toward the new French music had begun to turn at the time of the first trial of the *Damoiselle.* A leading critic wrote then:

"It is extremely modern and very fascinating. . . . Pages of sparkling, exquisite beauty. How refreshing is the touch of youth! . . . New blood such as his is just what this venerable society needs."

"New blood! The touch of youth!" It was the trumpet call not only for Claude Debussy but also for the others who would emerge in the dawn of modern French music. Chabrier and Lalo, a generation or more older than Debussy, were already known; Fauré, Dukas, and Duparc came later. Claude's contemporaries were Chausson, Pierné, and Charpentier. Ravel was thirteen years younger. In the short space of twenty-five years the new French school achieved fame and permanence. Today their names are alive and much-loved on our concert programs—as familiar as Bach, Beethoven, or Mozart.

Of equal stature were to be the writers and poets of "new blood." They had the same daring, the same scorn of tradition, that has added luster to the names in the French literature of the period. But this stature was not to be attained without strife among opposing "schools." It was Paul Verlaine who thus defined the origin of the so-called Symbolist movement: "A certain number of young people, tired of always reading the same sad horrors called *Naturalistes,* and bored by the serenity of the *Parnassiens* [classicists] . . . ventured to read my verses, nearly all of them written outside of any school. . . . These verses pleased them. . . . Chance then ordained that it was the moment for me to bring out *Les Poètes maudits* [Poets Accursed]."

This volume assembled four poets—Rimbaud, Mallarmé, Corbière, and Verlaine himself. Their deriders threw at them the name of *décadents,* which they gaily adopted. Their admirers soon called them the *symbolistes,* believing that a new mode had been initiated, in which "beautiful verses are exhaled like sounds or perfumes," in which nature is revealed through one's inmost self, where there is no oratory, no moralizing. First Baudelaire, then Mallarmé, Verlaine, Rimbaud, had "boldly elevated poetry to a vital plane."

The bookshop called "L'Art Indépendant" was a meeting place for some of the moderns, and Debussy would occasionally join them. While others talked he would listen, turning over the leaves of a book or examining an engraving. Or again he might seek stimulation at the house of Stéphane Mallarmé, whose Tuesday evenings were famous as a center for all those of advanced ideas. He lived in the rue de Rome, and Claude accepted his first invitation there with some reluctance, fearing that he might not feel at ease among so many brilliant intellects. But he was to find his way smoothed by the tact of his host, the "Prince of Poets" as his friends called him.

Mallarmé, his sensitive face chiseled by a rare and profound spirit, at once made his guest at home, and indicated the figures that could be dimly seen through the smoke of countless cigarettes.

"There in the corner is Paul Verlaine—the bald one with small eyes. Some have called him a dissolute vagabond. That may or may not be—but he writes beautiful verse. Wait—I seem to remember that while you were still a student you composed exquisite music for his *Mandoline.*"

Debussy, elated by this recognition, hastened to say that he had just finished another Verlaine group, *Ariettes oubliées.* Verlaine's mother-in-law, he added, had been his first piano teacher.

"Indeed?" Mallarmé responded politely, and went on. "Over there is the painter Manet, whose *'Dejeuner sur l'herbe'* caused so much excitement—you remember? Perhaps you know his portrait of me. And the slender *élégant* near you is the American painter, James McNeill Whistler. I regret that so far, Monsieur, I know too little of your music; but it has seemed to me that his art has the same exquisite delicacy I have felt in your compositions."

Claude knew Whistler's work and admired it; he thought he could discern in it a kinship with his own. From such encounters with contemporary artists and poets the seeds were sown that would flower in the music he would write during the ten years from 1887 to 1897. For one, there was Pierre Louÿs, who inspired the *Chansons de Bilitis,* and who gave him friendship of almost lifelong value by becoming a true intimate, and serving as a guide along the paths of his neglected cultural background and literary tastes.

Such were Claude Debussy's friends. Some quarreled and fought with him. Some left him, often to return and adore him. Against rivals and detractors he could always rally those who helped to stimulate his finest creative work.

12

"We should have music of our own, if possible
without sauerkraut."

O N A COLD MORNING in 1887, none too happy in the high
wind, Claude Debussy stood on a street corner looking
up at the walls of the Paris Conservatoire. His memories
of the place were neither fond nor sentimental. He recalled his
turbulent student days with their endless wrangling, and he was
glad they were far in his past.

Then he saw coming toward the school a distinguished figure,
white-bearded and walking with a cane. The younger man hastened
forward to greet Charles Gounod, now almost seventy. He had

always been Debussy's loyal friend and supporter, although they had not met in some time.

The Wagner vogue was then approaching delirium in Paris, a state of things that enraged Gounod. Musicians capitulated and imitated; writers were even more strongly influenced. French music as created by Gounod, Massenet, or Chabrier—all admired by Debussy—was giving way to pseudo-Wagnerian efforts. Debussy was well aware of Gounod's obsession, though he forgot it in the excitement of the encounter.

"Dear Master," he cried out enthusiastically, "I am enchanted to see you again!"

"And you, my dear young friend. What a pleasure! I hear much of your work. How does it go, the composition?" Then his always slumbering fury boiled to the surface. "What is to become of all music, all composition, with this abominable Wagner? You, at least, are not under his perfidious influence!"

Though Debussy could not truthfully deny the implication, he decided this was not the moment to acknowledge it. He did try to offer some defense of the Bayreuth master, but Gounod would have none of it. Gesturing violently with his cane, he poured forth a broadside of denunciation, ending: "There can be no possible argument!"

"But, Master," Debussy managed to interpose, "surely even you must acknowledge a genius—"

Gounod interrupted him abruptly. The final meeting between the coming composer and the composer of the past was over. He glared at Debussy and shouted angrily:

"*Pour toi, pour toi, pour toi!*" and stamped out of Debussy's life forever.

The violent episode was saddening to Achille, who had loved Gounod and owed him much. But what could be done about it?

A cherished friendship had ended that morning on a windy corner in Paris.

Debussy's worship of Wagner took him to the Bayreuth Festival in 1888 to hear *Parsifal* and *Meistersinger*. That year he was devout as ever; to him, *Parsifal* was like a religious rite. The frivolity of his companions, flirting with the waitresses during the long intermissions, revolted him. This was Debussy, the complete Wagnerite, at the age of twenty-six.

In the following year, 1889, his first doubts began to assert themselves when he went again to the Festival. His devotion had a sharp setback. He heard the same operas as in the previous season, and also *Tristan und Isolde,* first revealed to him in Vienna by Madame von Meck when he was only eighteen. Though he found his emotions still susceptible to parts of *Tristan,* his sharper critical sense began to discover what he considered defects in the idol of his youthful days.

As soon as he got back to Paris, Claude hastened to see Ernest Guiraud, his former professor at the Conservatoire and still one of his best friends. To Guiraud he pointed out what he called the "oppressive dramatic effects" in Wagner's music. He objected to the Master's use of the theater, rather than to his music. And he insisted that Wagner was overrated as an "innovator."

In this conversation with Guiraud he made one of those speeches that seem to have been instinctive with Debussy—almost clairvoyant:

"According to my conception, music begins where speech fails. Music is intended to convey the inexpressible. I should like her to appear as if emerging from the shadowy regions to which she would from time to time retire."

Guiraud's interest was at once aroused, and he asked what sort of poet Debussy would like to have write a libretto for him:

"One," he said, "who will only hint at things, and will thus enable me to graft my thought on his; one who will create characters whose history and abode belong to no particular time and place; one who will not despotically impose set scenes upon me, but will allow me, now and then, to outdo him in artistry and to perfect his work.

"And he need have no fear! I shall not follow the usual plan of the lyrical drama, in which the music predominates insolently, while the poetry is relegated to the background and smothered in elaborate musical trappings. There is too much singing in musical dramas. The characters should sing only when it is worth while."

Further encouraged by Guiraud, Debussy went on to describe his idea, with a pointed reference to Richard Wagner.

"My dream is to find poems that will not condemn me to perpetrate long, ponderous acts; poems that will provide me with changing scenes, varied as regards place and atmosphere, in which the characters will not argue, but will live their lives and work out their destinies."

Debussy made this expression of faith, which was to amount to a prophecy, in 1889, three years before he had even seen Maeterlinck's poetical play *Pelléas et Mélisande,* much less considered writing an opera for this tragedy. Yet how perfectly does Debussy's masterpiece fulfill his inspired prediction!

Debussy was a young Frenchman living in a city and in an age of freedom and of art. In such an environment it would not have been natural for him to confine his life solely to music. Romantic episodes began when he was very young; now they again played their part in his life.

According to the customs of his world, he had drifted into an informal association with Gabrielle Dupont, a very pretty blonde known to history as Gaby. It began with a chance meeting at a café. Perhaps the first attraction was "her mysterious, yet candid green eyes"—very arresting to one as partial to that color as Debussy. Often he would "borrow" a green tie from a friend, never to return it. And one of the songs composed at this time in the Verlaine group, *Ariettes oubliées,* bears the simple English title *Green.* In spite of the manner of their meeting, there was nothing frivolous about Gaby, and she held Debussy's devotion—though not exclusively—for the next ten years. It was interrupted once in 1893 by a brief, formal engagement to a young singer, Thérèse Roger, who had been a soloist in a performance of *The Blessed Damozel.*

But these episodes were mere detours in his life. It was, after all, to the green-eyed Gaby that he wrote a charming dedication in an early sketch for *The Afternoon of a Faun;* and also to her he inscribed his first studies for the opera he never completed, *Rodrigue et Chimène.* While it can hardly be said that he owed to Gaby any degree of musical stimulation, it is a fact that she was a help in many unobtrusive ways toward the end of their association, when he had begun work on *Pelléas et Mélisande.* René Peter, the boy of 1887 now grown to be a young man of the world and a close intimate in Claude's life, thus described Gaby:

"All the long months that he was always bent over the pages of his *Pelléas,* she went about with noiseless tread in order not to disturb the *chef-d'œuvre,* finding a hundred ways, smiles, and graces to deal with intrusive tradesmen; never hesitating at any kind of effort to maintain the daily routine of the household. . . . As for him, he did not descend from his heights except for the actual needs of life."

During his first years with Gabrielle Dupont, Debussy had been crystallizing his individual theories of composition. In 1891 he wrote to his intimate friend, the journalist Robert Godet: "Such music as mine has no other aim than to become part of things and people." There have not been many composers who could in so few words define the purpose of their creative art. It is clear that with Debussy convictions were succeeding doubts—to take form during the years soon to follow with the beginning of his masterpieces.

Debussy especially enjoyed expounding his views to that amazing character, Erik Satie, who was his friend for thirty years. The two were not only friends, but enjoyed working out musical combinations of their creative gifts. Few music-lovers who have heard it will forget Debussy's captivating orchestration of two of Satie's *Trois Gymnopédies.* Debussy had a passion for "arrangement"— piano pieces arranged for orchestra, or orchestra works for piano, two hands or four hands.

Like many another starving artist, Erik Satie, when Debussy first knew him, was pounding away at the piano and serving up café music at the "Auberge du Clou" in Montmartre. For a picture of this composer, here is a quotation from Satie's recollections:

"When I first met Debussy he was full of Mussorgsky and was deliberately seeking a way that was not easy to find. In this problem I was well in advance of him. I was not weighted down by the *Prix de Rome,* nor any other prizes, for I am a man like Adam (of Paradise) who never won a prize—a lazy fellow, no doubt."

Many pages have been written about Debussy and Satie—which influenced the other, who copied whom? The true situation can best be described, perhaps, by Satie's own statement: "If I didn't have Debussy I don't know what I would do to express my own wretched thoughts." And this is balanced by the certainty that Satie, on his part, was an active influence in leading Debussy away from what was left of the Wagner influence.

"I explained to him [Satie wrote] the need a Frenchman has to free himself from the Wagnerian venture, which didn't respond to our natural aspirations. I also pointed out that I was in no way anti-

Wagnerian, but that we should have a music of our own—*if possible without sauerkraut!*"

Satie loved to talk in that extravagant manner, just as he took delight in giving completely fantastic titles and instructions to his trifles for the piano . . . *Three Pieces in the Form of a Pear,* for instance, or *The Dreamy Fish,* or *Airs to Make You Run.* Performers are directed to play "on yellow velvet, dry as a cuckoo, light as an egg," "in the most profound silence," "with hands in the pockets," or "like a nightingale with a toothache."

Satie's own words about the music he wrote and Debussy wrote have come to the present author through an American writer, Dorothy Dudley. In 1925, seven years after Debussy's death, she was taken by the sculptor Brancusi to see Satie at the hospital during his last illness. Miss Dudley had protested, but Brancusi assured her that it would refresh him to meet an American who had loved his music from the early years. "When we arrived," as she recalls it, "Brancusi explained how back in 1906 my sisters and I used to go to the Concert Rouge where our favorite composer was 'Eric Satie-Claude Debussy,' as printed on the program. I said yes, that we were innocent about modern music, and for some time believed that our favorite was one and the same composer."

"Satie smiled vividly, almost had the strength to laugh. 'Yes,' he said, 'we collaborated . . . we found many sympathies in common. . . . Perhaps we were like complements.'

" 'Then you don't think Debussy is already out of fashion, as Brancusi seems to say?' I asked. As soon as the question was out I regretted it; it might tax his strength, so clearly ebbing. But no, a smile changed the lines of suffering, and Satie said slowly, each word an effort, but as if it gave him pleasure:

" 'Oh, our friend is wrong. Debussy will never go out of fashion.

We taught each other many things. Yes, we disputed often. The difference was that he created as if under the moon's rays, and I have wanted to create as if in the full light of the sun.'"

Satie was among the last of Debussy's "influences." His first, according to Madame von Meck in 1880, had been Massenet. She harped constantly on the subject when writing to Tchaikovsky about her "little Frenchman." And there were unquestionably others in his younger days. As for the various ladies of the first thirty years—Madame von Meck's daughter Sophie, his first small love; surely the fascinating Madame Vasnier, his first great love; and Gaby—each of these must have exercised an influence.

Certainly the painters of his period had a share in his development. His friends were full of talk about the canvases of Dégas and Toulouse-Lautrec, about the innovations of Renoir and Claude Monet. Chabrier was fascinated by Cézanne and Manet. Satie had said to Debussy:

"Why should we not utilize the methods that Claude Monet, Cézanne, Toulouse-Lautrec, and others have made known? Why could we not transpose these means into music? Nothing simpler. . . ."

No doubt the idea fascinated Debussy, though he never tried to apply it directly. Frequently he borrowed from the painters the titles for his works or suggestions for the manner of playing them. In one of his articles he quoted a famous saying of Baudelaire: "Perfumes, colors, and sounds correspond to one another."

Claude Debussy is often carelessly and incorrectly called an Impressionist. But he was not really of this famous school, being far less concerned than they with describing the impression made by particular scenes or moments. It was the essence of such scenes or moments, their soul as reflected in himself, that he sought to translate into musical images. In this, it was perhaps Cézanne that he was nearest to.

Debussy benefited by the interwoven pattern of all the arts, but his kinship was less with these painters than it was with the poets of his period—above all with those called the Symbolists. His deep preoccupation with Paul Verlaine, Charles Baudelaire, Stéphane Mallarmé, and Pierre Louÿs was a potent influence on a composer destined to illuminate the literature of this golden decade.

In his lifetime Claude Debussy wrote nearly sixty songs. The greater number of the most famous owe their inspiration to Verlaine. One of the first, *Mandoline* (dedicated to Madame Vasnier and written before receiving the *Prix de Rome*), is highly sophisticated and ironical for a young man of twenty-one. The same enchantress evoked songs for Verlaine's *Pantomime* and *Clair de lune*. Mary Garden, his first Mélisande, received the dedication of the Verlaine *Ariettes oubliées* of 1888.

In the same year Achille began to compose seriously for the piano. *Deux arabesques* still survives; little is heard of the five piano pieces brought out two years later. The *Petite suite* for piano duet of the same period was well liked, and *En bateau* from this group is so popular that it is often played in restaurants.

In 1891 he turned again to Verlaine in *Trois mélodies*. His dedications were less romantic; he favored Ernest Chausson and Robert Godet, possibly as advance payment for the many times they would have to listen to his troubles. Madame Godet was the composer's choice for the first of the three famous *Fêtes galantes* of 1892—*En sourdine*. He also revived his interest in his first poetic influence of 1880 with *Deux romances* for poems by Paul Bourget.

But before these he had composed the serious and challenging *Cinq poèmes de Baudelaire;* about ten years later the rarely beautiful music for *Chansons de Bilitis* by his friend Pierre Louÿs. And to

Stéphane Mallarmé he owed *L'Après-midi d'un faune*. More than any other French musician, Debussy became the anointed composer-laureate for the greatest French poets of his epoch. He understood best the elusive art of uniting their poems with the music that most precisely interpreted them.

V

13

"The ten years' work began slowly."

O N A WARM MAY NIGHT in 1893 the audience was drifting
out on the street after a performance at the Théâtre des
Bouffes Parisiens. Conspicuous in the moving throng was
the dark-bearded face of Claude Debussy. He was alone, and it
seemed plain that he was preoccupied. This was indeed true. Claude
was approaching the momentous decision of his life. He had just
seen a stage production of Maurice Maeterlinck's *Pelléas et Mélisande,* and had almost made up his mind to use this poetic drama
as the libretto for an opera.

The year before, he had bought a published version of the text,
and had made some sketches of incidental music for the play. But

now he gave these no further thought; he would lay them aside in favor of his new ambition.

Maeterlinck's play received scant approval; most of the reviewers were represented by the one who could not claim to understand its "unusual form and vague philosophy." But Claude Debussy knew that it was the libretto of his vision three years before. Later in his life he explained his choice:

"The drama of 'Pelléas,' which in spite of its fantastic atmosphere, contains much more humanity than the so-called documents of life, appeared to me admirably suited to my purpose. The sensitiveness of the suggestive language should be carried into the music and orchestral setting. . . . The characters of this drama endeavor to sing like real persons, and not in an arbitrary language built on antiquated traditions."

Here was assured conviction. Yet he had to contend with plenty of opposition among his friends, especially from his close adviser, Pierre Louÿs, who objected violently to his plan.

The ten years' work began slowly. In September he wrote to his devoted friend Ernest Chausson, to whom he often confided his perplexities or his successes: "Latest News: C. A. Debussy finishes a scene of *Pelléas et Mélisande* (A fountain in the park) on which he would like to have the opinion of E. Chausson."

By the next month he was not so optimistic, for he wrote:

"I was in too great a hurry to crow over *Pelléas et Mélisande,* for after a sleepless night, in which I began to see clearly, I had to admit I hadn't gotten things right at all . . . so I tore the whole thing up and struck off on a new line with a little compound of phrases I thought more characteristic. . . . Quite spontaneously I have used complete silence as a means of expression (don't laugh). It is perhaps the only means of bringing into relief the emotional value of a phrase."

The reference to "silence" shows that Debussy was intent on leaving behind all accepted forms, determined to make this work unlike any opera ever written.

He realized, however, that he must not get too deeply involved in the undertaking without procuring the permission of Maeterlinck, so he obtained from Henri de Régnier—a poet and novelist who was friendly with Debussy and Pierre Louÿs—a flattering letter of introduction to the Belgian dramatist:

"My friend Claude Debussy, who is a musician of the most clever and delicate talent, has begun charming music for *Pelléas et Mélisande,* which deliciously garlands the text while scrupulously respecting it. Before going further with this work, which is not inconsiderable, he would like authorization to continue."

Accompanied reluctantly by Pierre Louÿs, Debussy left Paris to travel to Maeterlinck's house in Ghent. On the way they stopped over in Brussels to call on Eugène Ysaÿe, the greatest violinist of the day. It was a memorable evening for the younger man. The immense Belgian hugged him against his chest and treated him like a little brother.

"And then music, and more music until we went mad with it," Debussy wrote to Chausson. "I played in succession the *Cinq poèmes* of Baudelaire, *La Damoiselle élue,* and parts of *Pelléas.* I got as hoarse as if I had been selling newspapers on the street. *Pelléas* softened the hearts of certain young people—English, I believe; as for Ysaÿe, he became delirious. I really can't repeat what he told me."

Though Debussy was thirty-one, he could still be excited by praise and recognition. Small wonder, when one recalls the years during which he encountered only academic censure!

From this gala evening of music the two pilgrims went on to Ghent and what they feared would be the difficult interview with Maurice Maeterlinck. But the dramatist, admitting freely that "he knew nothing of music," gave his cordial consent to Debussy's going ahead with his opera—a cordiality hard to reconcile with the shocking rows that were to occur before the first performance in 1902. To Chausson, Debussy described the meeting with Maeterlinck:

"At first he assumed the airs of a young girl being introduced to her future husband, but after some time thawed out and was very charming. When he spoke of the theater he seemed to me a very remarkable man. . . . He says he knows nothing about music. When I thanked him for entrusting me with *Pelléas* he insisted that it was he who should be grateful to me for setting it to music."

So now Debussy had his coveted libretto and must begin to work. But nothing further was heard from *Pelléas* that first year. Indeed, he was thirty-one when he began it—a young man; and over forty when he completed it. Always he found it hard to satisfy himself.

At this time Claude Debussy's troubles were not confined to *Pelléas;* they were also concerned with the problem of merely living. For what money he earned came only from hack jobs: piano lessons, transcriptions for publishers, and the like. The loyal Chausson therefore—always sympathetic—hurried around Paris to find him additional means of earning a competence.

The best of these engagements resulted from his reputation for playing the difficult Wagner scores on the piano—a specialty at which he had few equals. He took these assignments just as a small boy runs errands—to make a few francs. But he threw himself into the work with a ferocity that left him exhausted. It was his idea that in such playing he must not only constitute the entire orchestra, but at the same time indicate all the vocal parts!

Early in 1894 Debussy wrote to Chausson apologetically:
"It's Mélisande's fault—so will you forgive us both? I have spent days in pursuit of those fancies of which she is made. I had no courage to tell you all of it. Besides, you know what such struggles

are." And the next day, more gloom to be passed on to his friend: "The color of my soul is iron-gray and bats wheel about the steeple of my dreams. My only hope is in *Pelléas,* and God knows if that won't end in smoke."

The progress of his opera was marked by alternating enthusiasm and despair. A year later, however, he wrote to Robert Godet, asking him to note this historic date: *Pelléas* was finished! But the triumphant announcement was premature. Though Debussy thought he was satisfied, he quickly decided otherwise, and began once more to consider and alter the entire composition. Two years went by in this way before he reached the next milestone, the revised second version of *Pelléas;* by 1897 the mechanics of rewriting, at least, had been accomplished, but the composer's demands upon himself again upset him completely. He called the work "all wrong," and—but for the desperate entreaties of his friend Pierre Louÿs—would have destroyed the score.

During these troubled times there were long hard hours of work in the small flat on the rue de Londres. Claude was almost continuously at the piano; interrupting his concentration only to walk up and down the room, smoking endless cigarettes while trying to perfect a phrase. Luckily for him there was always the faithful Gaby to watch out for his comfort. She was completely happy in her humbler role of taking care of the housekeeping and making sure that he stopped long enough for lunch or dinner.

Often he sought his own form of "busman's holiday" at the home of Ernest Chausson. While the guests sat around the ornate little salon, Debussy with his coat off would thunder away at the upright piano, playing opera scores. Chausson leaned against the piano, following the music; the others sat entranced, dominated by the power he could always exert over appreciative listeners.

It was that year he wrote to Chausson: "Here I am, just turned thirty-one . . . and there are still things I am unable to do—create masterpieces for instance." Chausson answered dryly that Debussy knew perfectly well what he wanted.

So it proved. Within the space of about a year the composer created two undoubted masterpieces, permanent exhibits in the gallery of his works. The first was the String Quartet of 1893. Although it was marked *"Premier quatuor"* he never wrote another. It was played at a Société Nationale concert in December 1893 by his friend Ysaÿe, and three other eminent artists. The clash of opposing opinions resounded, inevitable with the appearance of a new Debussy composition. To Claude's bitter disappointment, Chausson failed him utterly, finding nothing good to say about it. "I was deeply grieved," Debussy wrote him. "I'll compose another for you, really for you"—but he never did.

On the other hand, the composer Paul Dukas, a loyal friend from the years at the Villa Medici, said of a later performance of the quartet:

"Everything is clearly and concisely drawn, although the form is extremely free. The melodic essence of the work is concentrated, but of a rich flavor . . . successions of rich chords which are dissonant without being crude."

Today we hear no talk of those "dissonant chords," and the quartet's lovely melodies enchant the modern audience. In the repertoire of every serious chamber-music group, the work is as obligatory as most of the classics.

The second masterpiece? On December 22, 1894, Paris heard *Prélude à l'après-midi d'un faune,* conducted by Gustave Doret under the auspices of the Société Nationale. Its reception has been given varying reports. One authority wrote that there was no enthusiasm in the press, and few would admit any superiority over the seven other numbers on the orchestral program. "One waits in vain for any heart or strength," another wrote. "It is precious, subtle, and indifferent in the same way as the work of Stéphane Mallarmé." But Léon Vallas, author of two standard books about Debussy, says flatly that "this little composition was such a brilliant and immediate success that the conductor had to repeat it."

In choosing the Mallarmé poem, Debussy had said: "It is not a libretto, but just an inspiration to dream about it." That his interpretation was entirely acceptable to the symbolist poet is shown by a letter Debussy wrote in 1910:

"I used to live then in a little furnished flat in the rue de Londres. . . . Mallarmé came in with his prophetic air and his Scotch plaid around him. After listening to it he remained silent for a long time; then said: 'I didn't expect to hear anything like that. This music draws out the emotion of my poem, and gives it a warmer background than color.' "

After such a tribute, Debussy could not be unduly disturbed by reviewer bickerings over his "Faun." They seemed inconsequential; the work had received its accolade. "One of the major miracles of musical history," it has been called by Oscar Thompson.* He is right. After fifty years the *Prélude* is frequently performed in this country and is one of the most popular of his four works for orchestra.

And on records, and over the radio! Many a time, through an open window the musical passer-by will be arrested by that enchanting phrase for the flute that begins *The Afternoon of a Faun*.

In spite of the continuing demands of *Pelléas,* of the labor involved in finishing the Quartet and the *Prélude,* the inspired interpreter of French poetry was not idle during his most prolific ten years. For one group of songs he became his own poet—the

* American music critic and editor who wrote a biography of Debussy (1937).

Proses lyriques of 1892-93. *De rêve* is a dream of the past, of the quest for the Grail; *De grève* compares the waves to frightened little girls rushing from school; the fourth, *De soir,* "Sunday in the cities, Sunday in the hearts . . . excursion trains, tunnels, signals."

Beautiful though these songs have been called, in greater renown today are the three *Chansons de Bilitis* of 1897. Created in the imagination of Debussy's friend Pierre Louÿs, Bilitis was a mythological enchantress who lived by the Aegean Sea. The songs are considered perfect examples of Debussy's genius in joining inspired verse with voice and piano. And, like the best of other Debussy songs, their subtle variations and difficult intervals are only for the most gifted artists.

14
"I've moved and I'm married."

THE PATRON of the Brasserie Pousset was languidly wiping his
zinc bar, when voices and laughter outside his door brought
him to quick attention. Then half a dozen young men and
women in gala mood entered. Certainly, he thought, this is something of an event. He hastened toward the dark one, whom he knew
well.

"Ah, bonjour, Monsieur Debussy. Messieurs et dames."

"Bonjour, patron," Claude exclaimed heartily. "Permit me to
introduce you to Madame Claude Debussy. The others you know.
We have come to your admirable restaurant for our wedding break-
fast. Fortunately, having given a piano lesson this morning I have

money to pay for one of your best. Afterward, we shall all go to the circus."

The *patron,* enchanted by the honor, hurried away to prepare an elaborate meal. He decided to offer two bottles of special champagne with his compliments.

The day of Claude Debussy's marriage to Rosalie Texier was October 19, 1899. She came from solid bourgeois stock in Burgundy, and had worked for a Paris dressmaker. Claude's friends have described her as "a pretty girl, with pale complexion, a small mouth, . . . rather dark brown hair." Her new husband wrote a charming description of his bride to Robert Godet, the recipient of so many of his bulletins of progress:

"I've moved and I'm married. Yes, my dear friend, and please remain seated. Mlle. Lily Texier has changed her name to Lily Debussy, much more euphonious. . . . She is incredibly fair; pretty as a legend. To these gifts she adds that of being not in the least 'modern style.' She . . . likes music according to her fancy. Her favorite song is a round in which it is a question of a little grenadier with scarlet cheeks, who wears his hat over his ear like an old trooper."

The ten-year relationship with Gaby Dupont in the rue de Londres and the rue Gustav-Doré was ended. On the fifth floor of 58 rue Cardinet, Debussy began another way of living considered more "suitable" to his growing importance in the world of music. The apartment had two high windows facing the street, and a balcony; his favorite color, green, prevailed in the decoration. Gaby's green eyes were forgotten for the stolen green necktie that the new Rosalie wore for a hat band.

For five years she was another devoted helpmeet, treating her husband like the "great child" that he was—difficult and capricious. She did her valiant best to keep a semblance of order in his life, to divert him from his bohemian ways into the life of domesticity led by her own class.

That Claude was very happy with his new wife is revealed by the dedication in the piece for orchestra he worked on during the first year of his marriage: "This manuscript belongs to my little Lily-Lilo. All rights reserved. It is proof of the deep and passionate joy I have in being her husband. . . . Claude Debussy, at the peep of January, 1901."

This was the orchestral work in three parts called *Nocturnes*. The first two "panels" of the triptych were given at the Concerts Lamoureux late in 1900; the final part, ten months later. It was amazing music and at once became another Debussy sensation.

Here was a composer who always disliked giving explanations that "destroy the mystery," but for *Nocturnes* he chose to put his ideas into illuminating words. Concerning *Nuages,* the first movement, he wrote:

"It renders the immutable aspect of the sky and the slow, solemn motion of the clouds, fading away in gray tones lightly tinged with white."

The second panel—that perpetual favorite, *Fêtes*—Debussy described in this way:

"It gives us the vibrating, dancing rhythm of the atmosphere, with sudden flashes of light. There is also the episode of the procession . . . which passes through the festive scene and becomes merged with it . . . with its blending of music and luminous dust."

In the third panel of *Nocturnes,* with a wordless chorus for women's voices added to the orchestra—*Sirènes*—he sought to depict "the sea and its countless rhythms . . . And presently, among the waves silvered by moonlight, is heard the mysterious song of the Sirens as they laugh and pass on."

One of the more intelligent critics, Gaston Garraud, took special care to define Debussy's intentions in *Nocturnes,* and to hail his arrival as a dominant figure in modern French music:

"He is one of those musicians—rare in any epoch—who impress one as being endowed with a spontaneous originality, and whom it is difficult to connect with any of his predecessors. Guided by a refined and unerring taste, he knows how to combine harmonies and timbres in ever-changing ratio. . . . Today he seems to have attained complete lucidity of thought and accuracy of expression."

In these uncompromising words the perceptive Garraud disposed of the critics who remained irritated because they could not classify Debussy to their own satisfaction, and equally of the reactionary musicians who scornfully tried to excommunicate him. Garraud knew that in 1901, at the age of thirty-nine, Claude Debussy had established his leadership in spite of all detractors.

Some time around the year 1898 Debussy had persuaded himself that *Pelléas et Mélisande* was really finished. It was submitted to Albert Carré, head of the Opéra Comique in Paris, who accepted the opera, though his interest was diluted by misgivings over its radical departure from every operatic tradition. The composer, however, was still not satisfied with his score. He took it back repeatedly for "improvements." Between Debussy's uncertainties and the management's apprehension, it was 1901 before *Pelléas* was scheduled for production.

The opera was to be directed by André Messager, a musician of courage who greatly admired Debussy and was proud to undertake the first performance. He has described the first reading of the score at his house before the singers engaged for the cast:

"The impression produced by his music that day was, I think, a unique experience. Debussy played his score at the piano, and sang all the roles in that deep sepulchral voice of his, but with an expression that grew more and more irresistible.

"At first there was an atmosphere of distrust and antagonism; then gradually their attention was caught and held; little by little emotion overcame them. . . . The last notes of Mélisande's death scene fell amidst silence and tears. At the end they were carried away, and eager to set to work at once."

Before preparations could go very far, they were interrupted by a dramatic episode calculated to shatter the nerves of any composer on the brink of a formidable ordeal. It took the form of a crisis with the very poet who had so gratefully provided Debussy with his ideal libretto. Maeterlinck had his heart set on having the role of Mélisande created by his wife, who had played that part in the original play. As Georgette Leblanc, she was known as an excellent actress, but not as a gifted singer. Debussy agreed with the arrangement, but without informing him the director decided against her and engaged Mary Garden. Though Madame Leblanc realized that Debussy was not to blame, her husband refused to believe it. In her account of the "scandal" she wrote:

"Maeterlinck brandished his cane and announced to me that he was going to 'give Debussy a drubbing to teach him what was what.'. . . I waited in agony, convinced of disaster. . . . I watched the deserted street for his return. Finally he appeared at the top of the hill, flourishing the cane to heaven with comic gestures.

"He told me that as soon as he entered the salon he had threatened Debussy, who dropped into a chair, while Madame Debussy distractedly ran toward her husband with smelling salts. She had begged the poet to go away, and, my word, there was nothing else to do.

"Maeterlinck, who did not like musicians any more than music, kept saying as he laughed: 'They're all crazy, all off their heads, these musicians!'"

Maeterlinck sought relief from his rage in a savage letter to *Figaro,* washing his hands of any connection with the project, complaining of the liberties taken with his work, and ending with a wish for "its immediate and complete failure." There was talk of a duel, but the affair was presently forgotten in the fever of preparation;

the first performance would take place without the support or presence of the author of Debussy's inspiration. Maeterlinck never heard the opera until many years afterward in New York, and then only one act!

The Maeterlinck quarrel was only one of the difficulties that intensified the arduous work of the rehearsals begun in January. In the cast, besides Mary Garden, were Hector Dufranne as Golaud, Vieuille as the blind king Arkel, and Gerville-Réache as the queen. They were devoted artists, consecrated to achieving perfection, but they felt the strain of perfecting vocal parts of unheard-of difficulty. In the orchestra the musicians grew exasperated over the badly copied music, the many rehearsals, and a score they considered unplayable and outrageous.

For Debussy there were inconceivable hardships in these final weeks. Always harassed by the changes he felt were demanded, or that were thought advisable by the directorate, he toiled over his revisions until the last moment before the dress-rehearsal. And right through the agonizing period of torment inevitable to a man of his hypersensitive nature, he was pursued by daily summonses on a debt he owed to the estate of a former benefactor!

By a beneficent miracle, however, composer, director, artists, and orchestra survived the ordeal. On April 27, 1902, Claude Debussy would realize the climax of his ten years of labor, the flowering of his genius in his one and immortal opera.

mostly unsympathetic to great poetry or great music. Even before the performance, trouble arose outside the theater, where a malicious fake program was being sold, ridiculing the entire work. Already Maeterlinck's public letter of protest had given Debussy's enemies a chance for a good laugh. However, the stupefaction created by the first scene drugged the audience into comparative calmness, and Scene II began.

The action of this scene was six months later. Geneviève, the mother of Golaud and his half-brother Pelléas, read to Arkel a letter from Golaud saying that he wished to bring home the strange, silent girl who had married him without understanding why. The ancient king, with a sympathetic perception beyond that of the others in the play, could not entirely approve of the marriage, but he contented himself by saying, "It may be that there never occurs any event that is useless." Fate!

And it was fate again that Pelléas, though intending to leave on a journey, was persuaded to remain at the gloomy castle to receive Golaud and his elusive bride. "I know nothing more about her," the prince had written, "than on the day of our first encounter."

In the third scene of the first act, Mélisande and Geneviève are in the dark gardens at twilight, watching the sails of a departing ship. There, Pelléas joins them, and they listen to the songs of the sailors as they put out to sea. . . . In the morning, Pelléas says, perhaps he also must go. "Oh, why do you go?" Mélisande asks faintly. . . . Now it is dark, they must leave the gardens. Together, Pelléas and Mélisande make their way among the brooding trees to Golaud and Arkel, and the act ends.

During the first intermission, riots and disorders broke out in earnest. To most of the audience the whole performance seemed incredible, ridiculous—unendurable, in fact. It should be stopped! This was not opera; this was not singing. Here were no showy arias to permit a prima donna or a tenor to rush to the footlights and bring down the house with a sustained high C!

Where was the entertainment, the drama, in such shadowy characters and subdued phrases? These strange people moved around the stage, delivering the lucid recitative in a manner more like ordinary conversation. The fact that the listeners could follow the story from this clear diction seemed only to enrage them the more. And actually there were frequent moments of entire silence! Fantastic! Unforgivable! So, before an audience growing always more resentful, the second act began.

This time the curtain rose on clear sunshine, a lovely park with splashing fountains—a picture of youth and gaiety. Pelléas had not gone; he and Mélisande were laughing beside a fountain, like children with their playthings. They talked inconsequentially, always skirting the subject of love.

But, alas, Mélisande's plaything is the wedding ring given her by Golaud. Perversely, she keeps tossing it into the air and catching it—until it goes "too high into the rays of the sun." This time the ring is not caught and falls far down into the water. Mélisande shows little concern over the mishap, Pelléas even less. "It is naught," he says; "perhaps the ring will be recovered. If not, no doubt we can find you another."

The mishap was more than that—it was a symbol. In the next scene Golaud, lying in bed injured, reveals by chance to Mélisande that he was thrown from his horse at the stroke of twelve—the very moment (as she now recalls) that the ring was lost! Her evident depression moves Golaud to unusual sympathy, and he seeks to ascertain the cause. To question after question she gives but vague answers. In an effort to distract him, she flutters over his bed until he sees that her ring finger is bare! She stammers futile explanations, none of them the truth. All Golaud's tenderness has vanished. He grows furious, violently commanding her to search for the ring.

"Go at once and find it," he thunders from his bed. Then ironically, he tells her to take Pelléas with her to help her!

So for no reason except to pacify Golaud, Mélisande leads Pelléas to a dark grotto, far down in the depths of the castle. Naturally, no ring is there, but only three old paupers lying silently in the darkness. Terrified, the two hurry quickly away from the sinister cave.

It was during the scene with Golaud that one line had touched off the audience to uncontrolled derision. Mary Garden, the Mélisande, was then a comparatively unknown young Scottish-American singer. At the end, when she sang the pathetic phrase, *"Je ne suis pas heureuse"* ("I am not happy"), there was something about this understatement, delivered in Miss Garden's none-too-perfect accent, that was more than the listeners could endure. At the end of the act the yells and catcalls far exceeded the traditional uproar to be expected at the first performance of any important new work in Paris.

In the corridors there were almost fist fights between eminent writers and friends of Debussy, and his shrieking vilifiers. On the one side, battling against Debussy's enemies, were Henri de Régnier (who had introduced him to Maeterlinck), Octave Mirbeau, Pierre Louÿs, and Paul Valéry. . . . That the opera was even allowed to proceed to its end was due partly to the curiosity of the audience, but more to the devotion and courage of the cast. Beleaguered though they were, they continued to unfold the story with delicate and beautiful sympathy, undisturbed by the opposition.

Now came the third act and the famous balcony scene. Mélisande's beautiful hair, loosed from the window above, seems to drown Pelléas as he stands below reaching up for her hand. Love is open and admitted, and a rapturous dialogue follows; until the untimely arrival of Golaud, now suspicious, interrupts the enchanted moment. Trying to deceive himself, he says paternally, "Stop playing like this. . . . You are children, both of you." But Golaud is hard; a hunter and warrior, too old for Mélisande by many years. With suspicion, his jealousy mounts like a flame.

The tragedy darkens. In the next scene, for no apparent reason except to terrify his brother's imagination, Golaud takes Pelléas down to one of the gloomy vaults beneath the castle, and shows him the stagnating water at the bottom of a deep chasm. . . . Pelléas is relieved to emerge into the fresh air of the terrace again, but Golaud tells him sternly that he must have no more to do with Mélisande. The warning is disregarded. In the next scene the lovers meet again. The approach of tragedy is brooding over them, while Golaud keeps on watching and spying, building up his unreasoning fury.

Mélisande has found great comfort in the deep affection the venerable king feels for her. "An old man," Arkel tells her, "[must] keep on trusting in the freshness of life and drive away for a moment the menaces of death." But he can do little, for he feels that she is doomed. . . . This tender interlude is shattered by the entrance of Golaud, now quite beside himself. To Arkel he declaims passionately: "Do you see those great eyes? . . . I know them well, those eyes. I have seen them at work. Keep them shut, or I'll close them for many a day." He seizes the beautiful hair that has so enraptured Pelléas, forces her to her knees, shouting wildly: *"A gauche! A droite!"* as he twists the body of the sobbing, anguished girl from left to right, until the old king forces him to stop.

Now the story of the harassed lovers nears its end. Pelléas must go away and they can only meet for the last farewell. Their tryst in the moonlit wood is a climax of passion and despair, of desperate avowals. Then they hear Golaud creeping through the trees; they see him standing at "the end of their shadows." From these shadows the avenger of honor rushes upon the terrified pair and runs his sword through his own brother. It is medieval and ruthless. It is his law. And it brings him nothing!

For Mélisande, fleeing blindly from the scene of death, is seen in the last act lying in her bed in the castle. No longer interested in living, she is drifting to the end of her own life. Golaud, now over-powered by abject remorse, tries to save her, begs her to live—for what? Even dying, he gives her no peace; he torments her with questions, repeated over and over, always on the same theme: had she really loved Pelléas? What can Mélisande answer? Her search after love had been her guide, and she had always been thwarted—except for those few brief sunlit or moonlit moments that were against Golaud's law.

16

"Today or tomorrow, Claude Debussy's music will prevail."

THE FIRST PERFORMANCE of *Pelléas* owed much of its poignancy to Mary Garden's Mélisande. She merged herself into the role with a truth and clarity that have seldom been realized by any other artist. Debussy was enraptured by her interpretation. It was not until six years later that his impressions of the epochal dress-rehearsal were recorded. For the journal *Musica* he wrote:

"At last we came to the fifth act and I cannot describe the amazement I experienced. That was indeed the gentle voice I had heard in my inmost soul, with its faltering tenderness, the captivating charm I had hardly dared hope for, and which has since forced the public to acclaim the name of Mary Garden with ever-increasing fervor."

This was the same fabulous Mary Garden, then almost unknown in this country, who in 1908 led the company that first introduced her type of French opera to America. She became "our Mary" to the parents of the present younger generation; she taught them to know *Pelléas,* and also three Massenet operas: *Thaïs, Don Quichotte,* and *Le Jongleur de Notre Dame.* She gave her own fascinating interpretation of the heroine of Charpentier's *Louise,* an opera cordially hated by Debussy. If he resented her appearance in this role he must have forgiven her, for he went on to say in the article just quoted: "I hardly ever had to make any remark to her; little by little the character of Mélisande took shape, and I waited with a strange confidence mingled with curiosity."

What of the reception of *Pelléas et Mélisande* by the critics, the enemies and the friends of the composer, by the public? Again Debussy was a storm center of tempestuous winds that blew in all directions. There were a few eulogies and many more articles in the familiar vein of scorn. Some were kind enough to admit bewilderment only; the prevailing verdict was along the line taken by the gentleman in the *Petit Journal:*

"All I heard was a series of harmonized sounds—I don't say harmonious —which succeeded one another uninterruptedly, without a single phrase, a single motif, a single accent, a single form, a single outline. And to this accompaniment, unnecessary singers droned out words, nothing but words."

It is sad to think that Claude Debussy must read such misguided, malicious comment about a great work on which he had spent ten years! The superficial article aroused the ire of one critical colleague who was a true prophet:

"There will be mirth in the halls of the Library the day our grand-children, in turning over dusty newspapers, come upon the articles after this first performance of *Pelléas*. *There will be mirth . . . but also amazement and shame!*"

The students at the Conservatoire of Debussy's boyhood were ardent supporters of the disturbing new opera—until the Director "so feared the pernicious influence of *Pelléas* that he forbade pupils of the composition class to see it!"

The controversy raged for weeks and months; for years. Since its first appearance in 1902, *Pelléas* has been the subject of hundreds of articles, studies, analyses, learned dissections—for and against, wor-shiping and outraged. Choosing from all of these, let us leave the judgment to Henry Bauer in *Figaro*:

"Today or tomorrow, Claude Debussy's music will prevail . . . this intensely artistic work, so youthful, pure, and tender, in which the subject, inspiration, and expression are so full of originality."

Or to Claude's famous contemporary, Vincent d'Indy, who began his article with the often-quoted sentence: "With the exception of bankers and politicians, I do not believe there is a sorrier or more useless calling in the world than that of critic." Then he went on to say of *Pelléas:*

"It is steeped in many-colored waves of music which enhance its de-sign, reveal its hidden meaning, and intensify its expression, while always allowing the words to be visible through the fluid element that envelops them."

Or finally to the composer himself, in two statements made at different times:

"For the past ten years, *Pelléas et Mélisande* has been my daily com-panion. I do not complain of this long labor. It has given me a joy, an intimate satisfaction, which no mere words, no criticism can diminish.

Besides, some of the writers have understood me perfectly and divined my intentions. . . ."

"I do not pretend to have discovered everything in *Pelléas;* but I have tried to trace a path that others may follow, . . . which will, perhaps, free dramatic music from the heavy yoke under which it has existed for so long."

Soon Debussy's work of genius began to move forward to inevitable acceptance. Stoutly defended by enlightened musicians, his masterpiece gained a better understanding by the public. Within a short time it became a box-office attraction, and a source—almost the first—of real income to Claude Debussy.

As the receipts began to mount, Claude wrote one of his characteristic notes to André Messager, who had gone to London after conducting the first performances:

"I forgot to tell you that we made 7400 francs last Friday. You wouldn't believe the respect they have for me. The fact that I created *Pelléas* was of purely anecdotal significance, *but to have made money, that's what counts."*

Debussy's opera began to excite curiosity in other musical centers. Five or six years passed, however, before interest in these cities resulted in presentations of *Pelléas.* Early in 1907 Mary Garden again appeared as Mélisande in Brussels; the event was a sure success. Eight performances were devotedly attended during one month. The Belgian novelist, Georges Ekhoud, said that in future the beautiful drama of his compatriot, Maeterlinck, should never be deprived of the "suave, subtle musical score with which the French composer has imbued and impregnated it."

The French composer was not to fare so well with his compatriots when for the first time the opera was given outside of Paris in 1908. In Lyons it was a complete failure, played for only three nights to half-empty houses. To offset this, the musical capitals put on splendid performances during the same two years, in Germany, America, England, and Italy. Always the reception by musical authorities was sharply varied.

In Germany, the press was divided. In Frankfort one reviewer heard nothing but "false relations," and he used such words as "outlandish" and "monstrosities." The public, saturated in Wagner, considered *Pelléas* "excessively restrained and depressingly colorless." There were the customary protests from the audience. But in Berlin and Munich the reviewers were fearless and enthusiastic. One of them paraphrased Schumann's famous tribute to Chopin: "Hats off, gentlemen. A genius!"

In 1908 Arturo Toscanini, still the idol of America forty years later, conducted the Italian début of Debussy's opera at La Scala in Milan. The evening became a struggle between the artists and the audience; the noise was so great at times that it was feared the curtain would have to be rung down. Only through the persistence of students from the Milan Conservatory were further performances possible.

In May 1909 *Pelléas* was first given in London; Debussy went over for the rehearsals, but did not see the performance. He wrote to Jacques Durand, his publisher and favorite confidant during the last part of his life:

"They demanded the composer for a quarter of an hour, but he was peacefully reposing at his hotel suspecting no such glory. The conductor telephoned me that the opera had an enormous success, such as had rarely been known in England."

The leading English newspapers were respectful and recorded no disturbance over Debussy's innovations. He was then more acceptable to England than to many of the Continental countries. Throughout the years from 1902 to 1909 when *Pelléas* was being introduced to these countries, it was always that way. Although Debussy had achieved a masterpiece, its eventual recognition was won in the face of opposition, obstacles, battles, and acrimonious injustice such as have not often hampered the progress of any other great composer.

Another conspicuous case of critical blindness occurred in the United States—in New York. Oscar Hammerstein brought most of the Paris cast of *Pelléas* to his Manhattan Opera House in 1908. It was a piece of daring on his part, the work being almost unknown here. The adroit manager, who believed sincerely in the greatness of the opera, succeeded in building up active advance interest among the curious—enlightened and otherwise. As a result the "strange new opera" received many columns in the New York papers on February 20, 1908.

But Hammerstein's courage failed to impress Henry E. Krehbiel, then a truly distinguished reviewer on the *Tribune*. *Pelléas* was just too much for him! "Its success in Paris," he wrote, "is like that which any esthetic cult or pose may secure if diligently and ingeniously exploited. . . . It will now be in order for the gossips to speculate as to whether or not the work will be more than a nine days' wonder"—and a column or so more of thundering abuse.

(If Mr. Krehbiel had been allowed to live to a very old age, he would have seen the "nine days' wonder" still a success thirty-six years later in New York. In 1944 *Pelléas* was given with Bidu Sayao, Martial Singher, and Lawrence Tibbett before a sold-out house at the Metropolitan.)

Mr. Reginald De Koven, composer of *Robin Hood,* who in 1908 was writing for the *New York World,* was affected almost as badly as Mr. Krehbiel. But the gentlemen of the *Times* and *Evening Post* were more cautious and approached the subject with respect—even, in the case of the *Times,* with some admiration. The *Times* found "its beauty almost indefinably strange and unaccustomed, but it is very real . . . an endless orchestral stream of marvelous and delicate beauty. . . . It is by the shimmering and iridescent play and change of harmonic and orchestral color that the music has its most potent effect."

The scholarly *Evening Post* had this to say: "Debussy's work is so radically different from all other operas ever written that even if it is a masterwork (as its admirers contend) it will have to bide its time." Then he added the disproved statement: "Debussy abjured melody deliberately." Nowadays, countless measures of what are recognized as pure melody are heard in *La Mer, Nocturnes,* the Quartet, and the choral works—to mention only a few examples.

In its several seasons in Chicago, Boston, and Philadelphia, the Hammerstein company aroused new excitement among opera-goers. Its repertory was new to those accustomed to think of French opera in terms of *Carmen, Lakmé, Mignon, Faust,* or *Roméo et Juliette;* but *Pelléas* was generally accepted along with other novelties. Since that time there have been revivals of the opera when artists sufficiently gifted were available. Previous to its important return in 1944, a number of years ago Lucrezia Bori was heard as Mélisande, with the present dignified director of the Metropolitan, Edward Johnson, as an ardent and persuasive Pelléas!

The story of the singers who helped establish Debussy's opera in this country should be finished on a contemporary note. When Mary Garden left Paris for New York it was necessary to find another Mélisande. The composer brought forward a slim and very young English girl who had already sung his songs to his complete satisfaction. Americans who saw her at the time described her as the perfect physical and spiritual embodiment of Debussy's fragile heroine. That he found her all that he could hope may be read in her own words:

"For my first lesson I was very quiet and nervous, and by the way he looked at me I think he was even more nervous at the prospect. . . . The rest of the story, of how he called to his wife to come and listen to the rehearsal, has been told many times. I studied the part of Mélisande with him every day over a period of five or six months.

"He was a most exacting teacher. I have been present when his uncontrollable temper got the better of him, much to the discomfort of several famous interpreters. Whether my temperament or the color of my voice had anything to do with it I do not know, but he never got angry with me or corrected me through all the lessons of *Pelléas*. . . . Like shades of color that are endless, so are the impressions left on my memory by his vivid personality."

And who was this so-favored interpreter? None other than the miraculous Maggie Teyte, who returned to America in 1945 to be reborn as an almost unparalleled figure in our musical world. Her recitals were mobbed, her radio appearances were listened to by thousands, her records are valued as song perfection. To Maggie Teyte has fallen the honor of bringing to us her "memory of his vivid personality." She interprets him with such rare artistry that Claude Debussy's songs now have an appreciation in America that they never before realized.

In the summer of 1947 the same "miraculous Maggie" talked to the present writer about her memories of Debussy during her first friendship with him. Miss Teyte seems immortal in her hold on youth; her gestures and the swift changes of her lovely, expressive face made it easy to imagine how sympathetically she worked with Debussy to perfect her Mélisande and to learn just how he wished his songs to be interpreted. She spoke first about two of the *Proses lyriques* for which Debussy had written the words:

"They are marvellous in the way they convey so realistically certain familiar mechanical sounds," she said. "I remember a little boy in the street near his house who said scornfully, 'He gets those funny noises because he hears the trains on the *Ceinture*.' The remark was an unconscious tribute. The 'Ceinture' was a belt railway that made a circle around Paris; the rattling little cars are given exact expression in *De soir* ... And in *De grève* [On the Sea-shore] you hear perfectly the veiled, reedlike tone of the bell-buoy in a misty expanse of sea . . ."

Her recollection of Debussy's appearance differs somewhat from his biographers', who have implied a man of wide, squat build. She remembers him more as a big man, who would have been tall if he had stood straight instead of letting the weight of his head and shoulders sink them into his body. But in one of his bursts of temper, she recalled, he could be truly a formidable and terrifying figure.

"There was the time," she said, "when he and I were in the artists' greenroom back of the stage in a Paris concert hall. In the auditorium his Quartet for strings was being played as part of the program, and we could hear it clearly. I saw that he was very disturbed, pacing up and down, and I wondered why he was so nervous. Then I realized that he was not nervous—he was in a mounting fury. He seemed to pull his body into a contortion with his arms; he was like a dragon breathing fire.

"After the Quartet was finished, the first violinist came into the room, deferential and anxious, hoping for a word of praise. He advanced a question, something like 'How was the performance, Master?', perhaps anticipating an enthusiastic embrace.

"Debussy faced the violinist, who was unquestionably an artist of standing. He uttered only one savage sentence: *'Vous avez joué comme des cochons!'* and turned his back on the stricken performer, who crept away without another word. I'm afraid he could be like that. There was nothing in his ruthless nature that allowed him to be polite or disguise his feelings about any performance he regarded as less than perfection."

She had another thought. "Debussy was 'dark' and complicated. It has always seemed to me that as a composer, he was most comparable to Edgar Allan Poe as a poet."

There was one critical question to ask Maggie Teyte about the two French composers now well known to the American public. "Twenty, forty, or sixty years from now, which will have the most secure position in musical history—Debussy or Ravel?" It was perhaps an unfair question, but she formed an answer after serious consideration. It was evident that she thought highly of Ravel, which was only natural.

"Well," she said, "there is no question that Debussy started it all; that he created the revolution in French music." Ravel, she thought, had written great music—his quartet, his pieces for orchestra, his songs. But Debussy's contribution to French art through his settings for the poetry written by the great French poets of his day was surely supreme in the understanding of their genius that he alone could have felt.

VI

17

"Endless memories . . . they are worth more than reality."

THE TRAIN at the *Gare de Lyon* in Paris was about to leave for Burgundy. Amid the confusion characteristic of French families setting off for their holidays, one group of four people was conspicuous. In white trousers and panama hat, Claude the husband bustled about collecting baskets and baggage; an unnecessary activity, for Lily knew just where everything was.

While he went to buy cigarettes, Lily calmly installed her father and mother in a third-class compartment. Four vacant seats were so completely filled with their belongings that equally laden travelers gave a discouraged look through the door and moved on to seek other places.

With Lily's parents, Claude was on his way for a visit to their home at Bichain in Burgundy. There he hoped to find rest and relaxation after the strain of the *Pelléas* performance.

While Debussy was at work in Bichain on his next orchestral piece, *La Mer,* he wrote to Messager:

"You perhaps do not know that I was destined for the fine life of a sailor and that it was only by chance that I was led away from it. But I still have a great passion for the sea. You will say that the ocean does not wash the hills of Burgundy and that what I am doing might be like painting a landscape in a studio. But I have endless memories, and in my opinion they are worth more than reality, which generally weighs down one's thoughts too heavily."

Even with the money he had made from *Pelléas,* Debussy was still hard put to it to earn an adequate living. His carelessness in financial matters found him always in trouble. He lacked practical sense about money, and his generous nature led him to share any good fortune freely with his friends.

In 1903, therefore, he welcomed his appointment as music critic on *Gil Blas.* One of his first assignments was to go to London to review the Wagner season at Covent Garden. He wrote only two articles—one a tribute to the great conductor, Hans Richter, and another—with many satirical allusions—to the Master of Bayreuth. For by this time his early worship of Richard Wagner was entirely forgotten.

During his first summer in Burgundy Debussy had the bad grace to complain of the success of *Pelléas!* He wrote to Jacques Durand that "the Opéra Comique is absurdly taking up much of my time, and this life of the theater disgusts and deadens me." He was less deadened than he imagined, for the compositions of the years 1902 and 1903 were among his most alive and vigorous works. It was then that he began to emerge as an inspired composer for the piano.

During his life he wrote over ninety piano pieces that have been the delight of all pianists able to interpret Debussy as he intended. Everything he now composed became more unmistakably *Debussy*. To this period belongs a charming group of three "prints" called *Estampes*. All based on popular music, they have been called "impressionist" pictures of the Orient, Spain, and the Ile de France. *Pagodes* has suggestions of the Javanese dancers Debussy saw at the Paris Exposition; *La Soirée dans Grenade* is in the Spanish manner—at which he excelled though he had never seen Spain. The Spanish composer Manuel de Falla, who died in 1946, called this work "characteristically Spanish down to its last details." The third of the *Estampes* was *Jardins sous la pluie,* using two French folk songs. When played the way Debussy wished, it is one of the most magical of all his piano pieces.

Although Claude had begun to write seriously for the piano as far back as 1890, some of his compositions seemed to take a number of years to reach publication—like the *Suite bergamasque,* not printed entirely until 1905: *Prelude, Menuet,* and *Passepied;* and *Clair de lune,* the first ambition of young pianists.

Two single pieces coming after *Estampes* in 1904 are characteristic Debussy—*Masques* and *L'Isle joyeuse,* the second full of gaiety, but "Heavens, how difficult to play," the composer said.

Claude Debussy at the age of forty-two had fewer money worries, and by all regular standards should have been ready to settle down to an orderly life as a successful composer.

But no; again there must be another—and this time final—change in his domestic life. In 1904, after five years with his Lily, he began to find her soup-making, slipper-bringing devotion stifling. Perhaps this was ungrateful, certainly it was inexcusable, but no genius can properly be measured by conventional rules. When a new love came into Claude's life, he was only too willing to embark on another marriage.

She was Emma Bardac, the wife of a prosperous banker, a beautiful singer and an intelligent, musical woman of the world. For the companionship that Claude now craved no one could have been more suitable. But the shift of affections was not easy or smooth, and was attended by many complications. Lily took it very hard— nor can she be blamed. She remarked acidly that her successor had appealed to Claude's well-known love of comfort and luxury, which undoubtedly did have something to do with it. It was true that for a time Madame Bardac was able to give the composer everything he enjoyed—especially good cooking! He would be free from worry, and she would protect his privacy and make sure he could work unhampered—something that had not always been possible in his life with Rosalie Texier.

The episode outraged all Paris and cost him many friends. "How could any man leave one so loving and devoted?" He was derided as a husband who sought ease of living at the cost of fidelity. Always indifferent to public opinion, however, Claude Debussy rode out the storm and gave all his time and strength to his compositions.

Before the marriage with Emma could be legally arranged he had dedicated to her a group of songs: the second series of *Fêtes galantes* to Verlaine poems—two of them light and charming, but the third, *Colloque sentimental,* in a mood of disillusionment. Soon after Emma Bardac became Emma Claude-Debussy, she again received a dedication of the songs (not completed until 1910) called *Le Promenoir des deux amants,* to poems of the era of Louis XIII by Tristan L'Hermite.

From this time Debussy, so far as is known, made no further detours from the straight road ahead. He seemed happy enough in this second marriage, apparently appreciating the life he enjoyed at a pleasant house on the Square Bois de Boulogne. Before and during the transition period from first to second wife, despite handicaps imposed by endless legal and other complications Debussy finished his third epic work for orchestra. The first thoughts of *La Mer* came with his visit to Lily's family in Burgundy; the public performance, after the marriage to Emma Bardac.

Like *Fêtes, La Mer* (finished at Eastbourne, England) was in three parts—three symphonic sketches; and it was introduced to the Paris public on October 15, 1905, at the Concerts Lamoureux. Now that *Pelléas* had triumphed, there had been considerable excitement over what Debussy might do next on the grand scale. But the first performance of *La Mer* did not evoke general enthusiasm. Many charged that it did not bear out the promise of its title— which was cruel to a composer who had loved the sea ever since his childhood days on the Mediterranean!

Even Debussy's loyal admirers expressed disappointment that the sketches were not agreeably reminiscent of the sea music in *Pelléas*. They could not accept the fact that it was never this composer's way to repeat himself. Always he strove to renew his art—to achieve the different. This intention did reach one reviewer out of many who felt otherwise:

"I consider that *La Mer* marks a new phase in his evolution; the inspiration is more robust, the colors are stronger, the lines are more definite. One has the impression that Debussy . . . has here condensed and clarified the sum total of his discoveries."

Two years later *La Mer* was still a cause of dissension. Toward the close of 1907 there were several performances conducted by the composer. On one of these afternoons Debussy walked out on the stage and looked toward the audience from heavy-lidded eyes, giving slight acknowledgment of the scattered applause that greeted his appearance. There was always a difference of opinion about

Debussy as an orchestral leader: some considered him stiff and uninspiring, others believed he showed "precision, authority and power." On this day, to his devoted adherents he was a personality of force, a genius sure of himself.

He started to conduct *La Mer*. But before the first movement ended, the music had been interrupted by jeers, hisses, and catcalls, and vulgar insults were hurled at the composer.

Debussy stopped the orchestra and turned to face the people with folded arms. His black eyes were now wide open and somber under his heavy hair. Without a word he stared contemptuously at the audience, holding them until the noise-makers were virtually hypnotized into silence.

Then he turned back to his orchestra and with one swift stroke of his baton brought the men from confusion to alert attention. Once more the sea rolled and surged in triumph. There were no further interruptions that afternoon.

A month or so later, Debussy conducted *La Mer* in London, and his success was electric. With the exception of one droning disbeliever in the *Times,* there was hardly a protest.

At forty-six, Claude Debussy had arrived at the pinnacle of his fame—a fame that for the next several years brought inevitable consequences that he considered ridiculous. They took the form of Debussy cults, Debussy worship, strident and combative "Debussyism." Some of these fanatics wished to set him up as the leader of a "school"—which enraged him. "There are no more *schools* of music," he declared savagely. "The main business of musicians today is to avoid any kind of outside influences." When his friend René Peter protested that the Debussyists were getting on his nerves, Claude replied: "They are killing me."

He was pursued even from America. For several years a rich Boston lady, a persistent amateur, had besought him to write her a piece for the saxophone. She scattered commissions among other composers, but concentrated on Debussy with little result. It was impossible for him to write music to order, and he knew almost nothing about the technique of what he called "this aquatic instrument." He postponed and dallied until finally she came to France in pursuit and visited his home. "The Americans are very tenacious," he observed to André Messager. "The saxophone lady has arrived in Paris and is inquiring about her piece. Of course I assured her that with the exception of Rameses II, it is the only subject that occupies my thoughts."

To another friend he confided: "Considering that the *Rapsodie* [for saxophone] was ordered, paid for, and eaten more than a year ago, I realize I am behind with it. The saxophone is a reed instrument with whose habits I am not very well acquainted. . . . Her patience deserves reward."

But all that Mrs. Eliza Hall ever received was a rough, incomplete draft in 1911. Although he tried to be conscientious about her commission, he never could whip up interest in an instrument he considered "ungainly, and its use by a woman ridiculous."

Debussy had no intention of writing only one opera, and during the years after *Pelléas* (as well as before) he was constantly planning, sketching, and often beginning work on other operas. The dramatic form appealed to him. In all he considered five other operas.

From his youth he had been attracted by *As You Like It* and the idea remained in his mind throughout his life, without taking tangible form. Edgar Allan Poe was another great poet who fascinated him, and he adapted "The Devil in the Belfry" and "The Fall of the House of Usher" to librettos. He went deeply into the possibilities of a *Tristan,* to be altogether different from Wagner's; an *Orpheus,* which would have been nothing like Gluck's.

The success of *Pelléas* in New York at a rival opera house aroused the active interest of Gatti-Casazza, then director of the Metropolitan, who had produced *Pelléas* in Milan that spring. He came over to see the composer in Paris, hoping to buy the copyrights of the projected *Tristan,* "The Devil in the Belfry," and "The House of Usher." Those who had heard parts of them had said: " 'The House of Usher' would have opened to us an impalpable cathedral of sounds." Everywhere in the world of music there was impatience for new works for the operatic stage by the composer of *Pelléas.* Gatti was a shrewd impresario who wanted to get there first.

Claude told him that he had nothing written but rough sketches. Gatti persisted, and a vague contract was executed, with an advance that Debussy insisted should be a modest one. "Don't forget," he said, "that I am a lazy composer and that I sometimes require weeks to decide between two chords. Remember also that you are the one who insisted on making this agreement, and probably you will not receive anything. . . ."

Gatti-Casazza came to Paris from New York at intervals during several years, but never got his operas. Not one was completed.

18

"He gave the listener music, not piano-playing."

COME, *mignonne*, let me place you here on this chair. Now you shall listen to some very pretty music your father has written especially for his little Chou-chou."

His little Chou-chou was Claude's only child, christened with the names of both parents—Claude-Emma. Only three at this time, she could hardly comprehend the proposed treat, but she felt the excitement all small children show when an indulgent relative begins any activity before their wondering eyes. Hers were now staring at her papa as he sat down at the piano.

Graduated to fatherhood, the composer was delighted with his new role. Not that Mademoiselle Claude-Emma Debussy had shown any signs of becoming a musical prodigy; but her father truly loved her, and regarded her as the fulfillment of his fondest hopes. He now proposed to play for her from his new group called the *Children's Corner.*

First "Jimbo's Lullaby." Chou-chou owned an elephant doll named Jimbo,* and the first slow ponderous notes from the bass seemed to carry a picture to her childish mind. Her father was rewarded when her face lighted up with a happy smile. When the short piece was finished he said: "So that pleases you, darling. Listen then to another—the 'Golliwog's Cake-walk,' in which your father pays tribute to what the Americans call ragtime."

The child could not follow these strange words, but she understood the infectious rhythm. She began to sway and wave her hands more or less in time to the music. She exclaimed:

"C'est jolie, papa! C'est charmant," clapping softly. At this moment her mother came in, and Debussy turned to her proudly.

"See, my dear, how this little angel loves and understands her father's music. What an intelligent critic!"

When the suite of six pieces was published in 1908 it bore this dedication:

"To my dear little Chou-chou, with her father's affectionate apologies for what follows."

Those first years of Debussy's new marriage and fatherhood were notable for his further activity as an inspired composer for the piano. Before the *Children's Corner* came the first series of *Images,* comprising *Reflets dans l'eau, Hommage à Rameau* and *Mouvement.* "I think I may say without undue pride," he wrote to the publisher, "that I believe these pieces will live and take their place in piano literature."

* Possibly a French corruption of "Jumbo," the name of Barnum's famous elephant of the 1880's.

He was right. His best interpreters still find delight in the delicate, floating harmonies that illustrate the title of the first; the "gentle majesty of proportions" in the *Hommage* to the early French composer whom Debussy greatly admired; the gaiety, the humor and exhilaration so evident in *Mouvement.*

After he began the *Children's Corner,* and before it was published, he wrote a second group of *Images,* sometimes described as having more "condensation of substance and simplicity than the first." Of the three pieces, *Poissons d'or* appears most frequently on concert programs. Rather than literally suggesting goldfish swimming in a pool, it is considered a reflection of the composer's partiality for Japanese art that he had felt since his early days as a student in Rome. It is a brilliant fantasy, beloved by all artists who have the delicacy of touch to disclose its intimate beauty.

In 1910, Debussy seemed to have enjoyed himself especially in creating a pianistic trifle—inconsequential, some think—a waltz he called *La plus que lente.* Perhaps for that very reason it pleased him. "I think I will arrange it for orchestra," he wrote. "For the countless five-o'clock tea parties frequented by beautiful listeners of whom I have memories."

In 1910 also occurred a memorable meeting between Debussy and one of his most gifted exponents on the piano. First in America to recognize the new genius, George Copeland today stands apart among pianists for his devotion to Debussy's compositions and for his rarely beautiful interpretation of them. But he had not met the composer until the early summer of that year in Paris. Fortunately, he remembers their first meeting so well that recently he was able to describe every illuminating detail.

Mr. Copeland had never made any effort to see Debussy; he was afraid that something in the personality of the man might cloud his loyalty to the composer. Debussy was known to be difficult with strangers, and indifferent to what any artist had done for his music. But a talented musical amateur in Paris was acquainted with both men, and she induced Copeland to let her arrange a meeting at the small house on the Square Bois de Boulogne.

They were ushered into that same long salon on the first floor where Chou-chou's father had introduced her to her *Children's Corner*. Except for the grand piano, there were not many pieces of furniture, and through the deep windows at the back they could see a charming green garden.

After a short time Debussy came into the room. He spoke politely to the lady, and seemed to await the purpose of the call.

"May I present Mr. George Copeland," she said. "It is he who first introduced your piano music to America."

Debussy looked directly at the American for the first time, and offered only one word—"Really?"

The laconic response pleased Copeland, who disliked trite conventionalities.

Then there was a brief silence while Debussy walked the length of the room and sat down by a window, rolling a cigarette. To relieve the tension the pianist took charge of the situation.

"Shall I play something?" he asked.

"But of course."

"What for example? . . . Something Spanish?" The music of Granados, Albeniz, and Falla is another of this pianist's specialties.

"Certainly not," Debussy answered. "I am not interested in Spanish composers. I am interested only in Bach's music and my own."

Copeland considered the declaration more arrogant than exact, since it was well known that Debussy admired Manuel de Falla. But he decided to follow the composer's choice. The piano was covered with a heavy fabric, and he asked if he might remove it. "Certainly not," he was told.

Debussy

Copeland sat down and played ten of Debussy's piano pieces. After each he paused briefly; but the composer made no comment, and Copeland went on until he felt he had played enough. For several moments Debussy rolled another cigarette in silence. Then he said slowly:

"It is not my habit to pay compliments idly. But I have never thought to hear my music played as well as that in my lifetime. . . . But tell me, why do you play the first page of *Reflets dans l'eau* as you did?"

"Because I feel it that way," Copeland answered.

"I do not feel it that way, but you must continue to play the piece as *you* feel it."

With mutual understanding so quickly established, the two men met often during the next three months, always in the same room. They played for each other; Copeland considered Debussy a superb pianist. "At the piano he gave the listener music, not piano-playing —and there is a vast difference." Copeland was always entertained by the composer's scorn of many ideas prevailing in Paris at the time. It was the fashion to have all music express the personal, the romantic; every piece must have a "story." So Debussy was derided by some because his music concerned itself with the elements— light, air, water. Music, they insisted, must throb with "situations" —a theory that infuriated Debussy. One evening Copeland suggested that they go together to a performance of *Pelléas.*

"Why?" Debussy asked. "Let us rather go to *Tosca.* They now play *Pelléas* just as they play *Tosca.*"

After that year the American never saw the Frenchman again, but he has given us a vivid picture of Claude Debussy at the height of his career:

"Many people imagine that this creator of shimmering murmurs was a frail, vague, anemic individual . . . On the contrary he was big, very matter-of-fact, extremely witty, and most definite about everything. . . . One felt in his presence a man in complete control of himself."

19

" . . . people, landscapes, legends . . . incidents, stories . . ."

THE LAVENDER TWILIGHT of Paris shone faintly through the garden doors of the room where Debussy sought inspiration at his piano. In his mind was the old Breton legend: "When the sea is transparent in the morning light, out of the waves rises the cathedral of Ys, its bells tolling, its priests intoning; slowly to return to the depths where is resumed its enchanted sleep."

Massive chords rang against the walls. It was the climax of *The Submerged Cathedral,* once described as "the most beautiful piece for the piano since the last three sonatas of Beethoven." Certainly it is one of the more popular pieces of the first group of *Douze*

[143]

Préludes that Debussy perfected in the fruitful year of 1910. Four of them, including *La Cathédrale engloutie,* he intended to play at a concert in May.

Debussy wanted his "Twelve Preludes" to resemble no standard forms. All were very short, more like improvisations, and the title appeared at the end of each instead of the beginning. He called them "pages from a sketchbook, catching the life of some movement or form. . . . They should never be performed as a whole. Some of them are too intimate for a big concert hall."

It was Debussy's rare gift to feel the character of other countries almost as if they were his own; thus the first "Preludes" are fantasies of many lands. There is England in *Girl with Flaxen Hair;* Greece in *Dancers of Delphi;* the guitars of Spain in *The Interrupted Serenade;* Naples and the tarantella in *Les Collines d'Anacapri;* and America (some think) in the lively music-hall rhythms of *Minstrels.* With his second group in 1913, all the "Preludes" have been perfectly defined as "memories of people, landscapes, works of art, incidents, legends, poems, stories."

For the songs composed during this period, Debussy delved far into the past of his beloved France, to glorify an immortal poet of the 15th century. That François Villon was a vagabond, a thief, perhaps a murderer, in no way concerned this composer. He approached the genius of five centuries before with reverence only. In *Trois ballades de François Villon* the matchless interpreter of French poetry achieved the finest of memorials to Villon. They evoked this tribute from André Suarès, a writer of rare insight: "The masterpieces of poetry, for the most part, have no need of music; they have their own music. . . . But the genius of Claude Debussy is not wrecked in recreating these poems; it transposes them into another world."

Even the style of publication was treated with fastidious care, for he wanted the paper to have the appearance of parchment. "A day will come," he wrote his publisher, "when it will be withered, the music as well."

Time has erased his gloomy prophecy. The Villon songs, above all, the glittering, ironical *Ballade des femmes de Paris,* are the joy of all great artists—a monument for two men separated by so many centuries, united by the bonds of French elegance and French taste, "fine and piercing." A final word from Suarès: "He who feels this music with the spirit of love in which it was conceived will understand Debussy at last; and he will know not only the charm, but the veiled power and quiet majesty of his genius."

Majesty asserted itself in the piano music and songs of these years; and again in the fourth and last of Debussy's works for orchestra, *Images,* begun in 1906, finished in 1912. Here he said he was "trying to write something different—an effect of reality—what some foolishly call 'impressionism,' a term that is utterly misapplied."

Into the creation of *Images,* Debussy threw himself with enthusiasm. Like *La Mer,* it was a triptych; he named the three parts *Iberia, Rondes de printemps* (based on a French folk song), and *Gigues* (suggesting the style of English dances).

Today *Iberia* is the most frequently heard. The composer had never known Spain; he was writing not "Spanish music" but his imaginative idea of Spain. To a writer who wished to prepare program notes, he said: "It is useless to ask me for anecdotes about this work. There is no story attached to it, and I depend on the music alone to arouse the interest of the audience." Yet who could know the musical expression of Spain better than Manuel de Falla, who wrote:

"The intoxicating spell of Andalusian nights, the festive gaiety of a people dancing to the joyous strains of guitars . . . all this whirls in the air, approaches and recedes, and our imagination is continually dazzled by the power of an intensely expressive and richly varied music."

Early in 1911 Debussy was asked by the Italian poet Gabriele d'Annunzio to undertake incidental music for his new miracle play, *The Martyrdom of Saint Sebastian*. It was a project that appealed to the composer. He knew that d'Annunzio admired his music, and it offered another opportunity to write for the stage. On the other hand, he was disturbed by the need to do the work quickly. "It would take me months of concentration," he said, "to write adequate music for this subtle, mysterious drama. But I labor under the distressing obligation to have it ready by May."

The first indications of serious illness had already appeared; he was handicapped by increasing poor health. When the final score reached his publisher, Debussy wrote: "I admit I am not displeased with it. But as I have told you several times, I am at the end of my tether." In saying this, he was unfair to himself; Debussy was never "through"—he was a working composer almost to the end of his life.

Notwithstanding the promising combination of poet and musician, the public performance of *Le Martyre de Saint-Sébastien* (for solo voices, chorus, and orchestra) came close to failure. It was hampered by the strong resentment of the Archbishop of Paris, who saw religious desecration in the play and forbade Catholics to attend. And Ida Rubenstein, the famous dancer and mime who had commissioned the work for herself, proved an inadequate interpreter of the principal role.

The production was examined with the utmost seriousness by the critics, who found themselves in sharp disagreement. For an opinion on the music, appreciative yet fair, there is Gaston Garraud again. He had lost some of his confidence in Debussy, but now found it restored. He summed up his conclusions about *St. Sebastian* in these words:

"It impressed me as being one of the finest things Debussy has ever written. In spite of the sumptuous coloring and the fanciful originality and marvelous diversity of the instrumental combinations, the emotion of the essential work remains intensely spiritual and of a rare purity."

The "Martyrdom" was Debussy's first production on the stage after *Pelléas;* it cannot be said to have taken any place in musical history as a success. Nor can several other attempts he made at about the same time, directed toward the theater, or more especially the ballet theater.

One of these was a commission he was obliged to accept, for now he began to need money; his second wife was apparently not so rich as everyone had thought. When the English dancer Maud Allan asked for an Egyptian ballet, he tried to oblige, but with little heart for the job. It was never finished. Debussy himself made fun of the effort, "which suggests a riot," he said, "or an outbreak of fire, and gives one the shivers."

Another chance came with which he was far more sympathetic. André Hellé was an illustrator of children's books, and a ballet was being considered for his *Boîte à joujoux.* The notion of a toy box containing a human drama was just what would attract Debussy; when he wrote the music he always had in mind his adored little Chou-chou. To arrive at the childish level necessary, he said that he amused himself extracting confidences from some of her old dolls.

The Box of Toys was not produced until 1919, when it was received with delighted favor. Though very simple, and dismissed by its composer as a "small work to amuse children and nothing more," it was called a little masterpiece of French music.

His third approach to the stage was indirectly due to Diaghilev's Russian ballet, world-famous before Germany invaded France in 1914. Leading the troupe was the brilliant, flashing figure of the dancer Nijinsky, who sought to find a new ballet worthy of his genius.

With a journalist friend Debussy was sitting on the terrace of one of his favorite haunts, the Café Weber on the rue Royale. "Now this Nijinsky," he said scornfully, "wishes to make a ballet out of the *Afternoon of a Faun*. I am not in favor of it. I do not like him."

Nevertheless the dancer succeeded—without Debussy's consent—in putting on his version of the "Faun"; it prevailed in the repertoire of the Ballet Russe, even in several American performances. It became an accredited success and aroused popular interest, at least; but the experiment never pleased Debussy, who disposed of the Russian star in a letter to Robert Godet:

"Nijinsky's perverse genius is entirely devoted to peculiar mathematical processes. The man adds up in demisemiquavers, and proves the result with his arms. Then, as if suddenly stricken with partial paralysis, he stands listening to the music with a most baleful eye. It is ugly. . . ."

In spite of his prejudice, Debussy was persuaded to collaborate with Nijinsky in what seemed to be an idea of great promise. It was to be a ballet called *Jeux,* with scenario and choreography by the dancer. Nothing but the possible profits would have forced Debussy into the association, though the plan certainly attracted him. It was very pretty, suggesting a tennis game among three young people, and the search for a lost ball in the gardens at dusk. Debussy gave his best; the music was playful and ingenious, and contrived to convey the bounding effects of shots and volleys.

However, in spite of the music and the setting—both considered unusually charming by many reviewers—*Jeux* pleased only the select minority, not the general public. The failure of a work for which he had had great hopes could only depress any composer, especially one working under the physical handicaps that now beset Debussy more and more. It had become only too evident that his disease was cancer.

This has been an account of Debussy's notable range and variety of production during the compact period from 1910 to 1913. In it he produced major compositions for the piano, the voice, the orchestra, the stage, and the ballet; and his partiality for woodwind instruments led him to write a *Rapsodie* and a *Petite pièce* for clarinet and piano—test pieces for students, noteworthy for their understanding of the clarinet; and *Syrinx,* an exquisite little gem, only one page long, for unaccompanied flute. None were unworthy of their composer, no matter what place they hold today. They show his persistent devotion to exploration and experiment in wide fields of music.

A fitting postscript may be added. Debussy pulled himself out of his discouragement over the reception of *Jeux* to turn back to his favorite of twenty-six years before, Stéphane Mallarmé, now dead. To the poet's memory he dedicated *Trois Ballades de Stéphane Mallarmé.* They are profound songs, deeply searching in their interpretation of the poet, Debussy at his height as the "composer-laureate" of French poetry. So intricate is their imagery that as much depends on the listener as on the performer. His last songs, they are a noble tribute to the great poet who had given Debussy his inspiration for the *Prélude à l'après-midi d'un faune.*

VII

20

"My music aims at being nothing else but melody."

THE STORY of Claude Debussy's creative work in the three or four years following 1910 has been told. Unfortunately there is a parallel story, which for him was all too much a travelogue; after the first of many journeys he said: "I am not the composer to take my wares abroad. You have to have the heroism of a traveling salesman."

Visits to Austria, Hungary, Italy, Russia, Holland, Italy again, and the last to London in 1914, were compulsory. From these countries came repeated demands that Debussy conduct his works in their musical capitals. Even though it gratified his vanity, this alone

[153]

could not have moved him. It was the necessity of making money to pay for the luxuries which he craved and which the family assets could not provide. Otherwise he would have preferred the relative comfort and peace of his house near the Bois du Boulogne.

Debussy was right: travel exacts "heroism." It is not a happy picture to look back upon. Here was a very sick man, unable to afford a *wagon-lit;* he must make long night trips sitting up with a rug around him against the cold. Sleep could be only fitful, rest or relaxation a mockery. He reached his destination each time depleted and worn out—to face the ordeal of an appearance before a strange audience.

The chance to conduct an orchestra in his own music seldom elated him as it seems to elate many composers. He knew his limitations. "It's amusing while you seek out the colors at the end of the little stick," he said; "but after a time it's like an exhibition, and the greeting of the audience is not very different from that received by a showman in a circus."

The visits to Vienna and Budapest in 1910 turned out to be triumphs, even though in Vienna the time for rehearsal was all too short. Debussy was to conduct *Iberia* and *The Afternoon of a Faun,* the latter previously played in Vienna under the leadership of Richard Strauss. He wrote to Durand:

"I can assure you it was hard work to get *Iberia* into shape. I made use of every possible means of expression. I sang. I gesticulated like a character in an Italian pantomime. . . . Well, they managed to understand in the end, and I got what I wanted out of them. . . . At the performance I was recalled as often as a ballet dancer; the only reason the idolizing crowd did not unyoke the horses from my carriage was that I rode in a taxicab."

Debussy's reserved nature made him dislike exploitation and publicity, and he never quite enjoyed the elaborate receptions in his honor. Ill-advised compliments annoyed him; when a guest at a Vienna banquet tried to felicitate him on "abolishing melody," he answered: "But, Monsieur, my music aims at being nothing else but melody."

He had a better time in Budapest, as he recalled later in a letter to his oldest friend, Gabriel Pierné:

"The Hungarians are charming people; there is something French about their enthusiasm which brings us more quickly into sympathy with them than with our so-called Latin brothers."

His intuition proved exact when he went to Italy in June 1910. The trip from Paris to Turin tired him, following so closely on the strain of composing *St. Sebastian* in a few short weeks. He felt obliged to confide to the Italian director of the orchestra: "May I ask you, Monsieur, to take charge of the rehearsals? It is an ordeal I would rather avoid."

The conductor agreed politely, but wondered why the great man was willing to leave this important detail to another. His surprise was natural: the French composer had always been known for the elaborate care he bestowed on preparation, never sparing himself. By this time it was evident that his illness must be taken into account.

When the fine program of French works was presented, Debussy was unequal to a full demonstration of his power, and proved uninspiring to the orchestra. Music by Chabrier, Dukas, and Roger-Ducasse, with three of his own pieces, did not emerge as the hoped-for glorification of French music. "Debussy conducted as well as he could," one critic said afterwards, "but without control, and the performance failed to impress the audience."

Back again in Paris, the composer expressed himself philosophically to a newspaper interviewer:

"I was hissed in Italy; perhaps the day will come when I am applauded. We should not expect our works of art to be recognized in our own epoch. We do not write to become millionaires; we should be able to see a little farther than the end of a score."

Two years later, memories of the Italian failure were obliterated by the famous concerts in Russia, at that time still the empire of the Czars. In the interval Debussy's health had not improved—quite the contrary; but his partiality for Russia ever since the days of Madame von Meck now rekindled the fire of his genius to new heights.

In response to an invitation from Serge Koussevitsky * to conduct concerts of his own music, Debussy went to Moscow and St. Petersburg in December 1913. Before his arrival, rehearsals had been long and thorough; his audiences were in eager anticipation, and both concerts were a magnificent success. The Russians regarded Debussy as the "spiritual son of Rimsky-Korsakov and Mussorgsky, and as the one master of French art who had established a link between East and West."

Léon Vallas, whose two books on Claude Debussy and his music are an acknowledged authority, wrote of his command of the Russian audiences: "His face, which resembled that of a Byzantine ikon, his aloof manner, and his indifference to the public were all characteristics that helped to surround him with a halo. Although realizing that he lacked the requisite talents for a conductor, the musicians accorded an enthusiastic reception to his interpretation of his own works."

The day that Claude Debussy had diffidently predicted might come, "when I am applauded in Italy," achieved a brilliant reality at the Augusteo in Rome, in February 1914. In the city of his reluctant student days Debussy enjoyed a glory never imagined either by himself or by his teachers at the Villa Medici. It proved to be an atonement for the shabby treatment *Pelléas et Mélisande* had received in Italy years before. As always, there had to be protests

* Since 1925 the distinguished conductor of the Boston Symphony Orchestra.

and disorders on the part of antimodernists and nationalists, but they were overpowered by salvos of applause from the more intelligent members of the audience. The story of the triumph may best be told by a highly emotional writer in an Italian newspaper, *La Tribuna:*

"The nationalists regained their assurance and attempted a sudden attack. . . . There was a moment of tense anxiety. Fortunately Debussy did not allow himself to be intimidated. Secure in the knowledge of his coming victory, he turned and looked straight at his adversaries in the upper galleries; then in a spirited manner attacked *The Afternoon of a Faun.* It was indeed a victory—a brilliant one. As the work ended, the Augusteo shook with applause. It was a scene of delirium. Those of us who had feared for the good name of our city breathed a sigh of relief."

This was the last time Claude Debussy had to face hostile demonstrations. It was followed immediately by two concerts in Holland that served to establish forever an unchallenged supremacy; in the second half of each program he came forward as composer, conductor, and pianist. From the more phlegmatic Dutch, "delirium" could hardly be expected, but the programs in The Hague and Amsterdam won tributes that had dynamic consequences in Debussy's own country. The organizers of the concerts published his welcome to Holland:

"It is not surprising that this composer should have encountered implacable enemies as well as enthusiastic admirers. But he has never ceased to hold his own against all attacks; he has bravely accomplished his task and won the victory. Today he is recognized as an authority not only in France, but in the entire musical world."

Recognition as a great master in another country stirred some of the "Immortals" in the Institut de France several months later to make good the phrase "an authority not only in France." That summer a seat was vacant in the Académie des Beaux Arts; Debussy's adherents planned to propose him as a candidate. But proceedings were delayed by the violent opposition of Saint-Saëns, and several years dragged by without further action.

Debussy finished the cycle of his journeys abroad with one more appearance in London in June 1914. Again the need of money was urgent or nothing would have induced him to leave Paris, for he was now almost wholly in the grip of his fatal illness. Even at that, he wrote derisively of the compensation to Durand: "Caruso would demand for his accompanist the fee I am getting. . . . But at any rate it is a drop of water in the desert of these dreadful summer months."

In the last three words, Claude Debussy had no vision of the "dreadful summer months" that would overwhelm his beloved France in August 1914. Monarchs and diplomats may have foreseen the terror of that summer; but Debussy was writing lightly, with only his own financial worries in mind. Since early boyhood he had thought himself living in a secure world of international peace; a tranquillity inconceivable now to those who have watched one restless decade follow another since the First World War. How truly dreadful the summer months would be was then beyond the imagining of Debussy and his fellow countrymen.

21

"The voice has worn itself out."

DURING THE FIRST four swift days of August 1914 the appalling catastrophe burst over Europe. In just four days Claude Debussy and his compatriots must learn to believe the unbelievable—that their country was once more challenged by the German hordes!

But Claude of France (as d'Annunzio called him) could only watch helplessly while his countrymen flung the Tricolor to the winds of battle. He could only listen while they sang the *Marseillaise* of other wars, formed their battalions, and marched to face the invader.

For Debussy was now too ill, as he had been too young in 1870, to throw himself into the struggle. It was not that he sought the artist's privilege of standing aside. He was unfit in years and in body, and his increasing illness had weakened his spirit. To Durand, his publisher, he wrote frankly about his emotions during the first days of the invasion:

"You know I have no sang-froid and certainly nothing of the military spirit. I've never held a rifle in my hands. . . . All this makes life intense and troubled. What I am doing seems so wretchedly small. I've got to the state of envying Erik Satie, who as a corporal is really going to defend Paris."

His helpless situation disturbed him. In another letter he invented a grim alternative that happily never came to pass:

"My age and fitness allow me at least to guard a wall. But if, to secure victory, they are absolutely in need of another face to be bashed in, I will offer mine gladly."

What could he do for his beloved country? For the first terrible year of the war, very little. He arranged with Durand to edit the Valses and Polonaises of Chopin to replace the German editions. One composition was published, *Six épigraphes antiques,* for piano duet, regarded by Suarès (though not by several others) as among his greatest works. The year was one in which it was difficult for Debussy to bring himself to writing music.

At the end of 1914 he found a patriotic outlet in composing for "The King of the Belgians' Book" a *Berceuse héroïque,* written as a tribute to the soldier-king. He incorporated the *Brabançonne,* the national anthem, thus suggesting "the dismal trenches of Flanders, full of harassed, homesick soldiers who were soothed by the patriotic melody."

Soon he began to compose with his former strength and inspiration. "I want to work," he said, "not so much for myself, as to give proof, however small it may be, that even if there be thirty million

Boches, *French thought will not be destroyed.*" Under handicaps that would have defeated many a creative artist, he finished in 1915 the first two of what he hoped would be six sonatas for various instruments. They are beautiful and enduring compositions, vivified by what he considered his return to the French forms he now wished to exalt. In this new awakening to creation, they were written without effort—"the joy that fills the work is evident to all who hear it."

The first sonata is in the standard association of 'cello and piano: the second is a Debussy innovation for flute, viola, and harp, the only one of its kind. The coloring in this combination of instruments is so novel and inspired that the trio has a shimmering tenderness. "It is so terribly sad," Debussy wrote, "and I do not know whether one ought to laugh or cry at it. Perhaps both."

When this sonata was performed in New York thirty years after its composition, it moved an intelligent reviewer to write: "The Trio is not easy to blend, but the rewards of success are well worth the trouble they take. . . . The work is a dream of evanescent and auditory delights."

On the cover of the two sonatas Debussy used for the first time the self-conferred title, *Musicien français.* Its fitness cannot be questioned. In heart and spirit, Claude Debussy was the "Musician of France," and never more so than in the war years. The music he composed then was offered as a tribute to the youth of France, needlessly destroyed on the battlefields.

From Pourville, near Dieppe, he wrote during that summer that he had regained the capacity of thinking and writing. He composed three pieces, *In Black and White,* for the infrequent combination of two pianos, which have greatly enriched a limited repertory. And it amused him to compose twelve *Etudes* which he described as "a thousand different ways of treating pianists according to their just deserts."

"These *Etudes*," he wrote, "will be a useful warning to pianists not to take up the musical profession unless they have remarkable hands. The most minute Japanese engravings are child's play beside the transcription of some of these pages. . . . Yet there is no need to render technique more depressing for the sake of making a serious impression; a touch of charm has never spoiled anything. Chopin proved that."

At the end of 1915, with its constant strain of hard work, on the eve of an operation Debussy wrote his last song. It completed a galaxy of songs that are, as Oscar Thompson said, "the essence of Debussy's musical personality. . . . They exhibit virtually every facet of his art. There is nothing else like them in song literature." The last of about sixty songs, it is a simple piece of great beauty for which he also wrote the words. This small masterpiece, *Le Noël des enfants qui n'ont plus de maison,* shows his feeling for the pitiful plight of thousands of children made homeless in France and Belgium.

For almost a year Debussy composed nothing. The operation gave only temporary relief. He was a very sick man, and no one knew it better than he. But the tendency to be satirical about his condition never left him; his letters to Durand are graphic pictures of these few years. From the various places in the country where he sought recovery he wrote frequently; he said that he had made up his mind to ignore his tyrannical malady and would work in spite of everything: life was endurable only if he composed a great deal:

"As the days go by I must admit I am losing patience. Life has been too hard, and Claude Debussy, writing no more music, has no longer any right to exist. They never taught me anything but music. . . . If I am doomed to vanish soon, I desire at least to have done my duty. . . ."

In 1917 he wrote to Durand: "I am near the end of a life of waiting. My waiting-room existence I might call it—for I am a poor traveler waiting for a train that will never come now." But again Debussy was being hardly fair to his own courage, his determination to compose when he could and to appear before his people with French music composed for the French. He put his resolve into these words:

"I have come to the conclusion that, all things considered, it would be cowardice on my part to join the ranks of the disabled, and spend my time dwelling on the atrocities that have been committed. . . . Better to react against them by creating, to the best of my ability, a little of that beauty the enemy is attacking with such fury."

Claude Debussy finished his swan song, the sonata for violin and piano, in 1917. He gathered strength to play it twice with the violinist, Gaston Poulet: once in St.-Jean-de-Luz, and before that in Paris in his last public appearance as a composer-pianist.

The Paris world of music, in which he had so long been a commanding figure, an adored genius, and a storm center of controversy and opposition, saw Debussy for the last time in June 1917. He was in the audience at a French-Italian concert, where a splendid performance of *La Mer* was given.

He could have asked for nothing better as a farewell, for it *was* his farewell to the French people. He withdrew entirely from them. His indomitable spirit could do no more; his sickness condemned him to inaction. From the beginning of 1918 he had to stay in his room at the house near the Bois du Boulogne, with his wife in stricken attendance. "Always in bed, in bed!" he said to Louis Laloy, who came to see him. They were rehearsing *Castor et Pollux* at the Opéra. Laloy wrote, "One of his last regrets was not to be able to go. 'Remember me to Monsieur Castor,' he said feebly, trying to smile as I went off." Fortunately, Debussy was now too ill to suffer the further torture that would have come had he known of the desperate situation that confronted France in the first months of

1918. Nor was he to live long enough to share in the triumph of her final victory.

Nor could he finish the great patriotic work he had planned long before: an *Ode à la France* for solo voices, chorus, and orchestra. It had been his passionate hope to write this last great tribute to his country—on the grand scale; to take "Jeanne d'Arc as the personification of suffering France." Nor, finally, could he complete the *As You Like It* which he had so wanted to create. . . .

It is pitiful to think of the sufferings of this great man's last days. When finally he wanted to send in his letter of candidature for the Academy, his hand could scarcely manage a trembling signature; the Institut de France would never have the glory of his living name.

Now far too ill even to be carried down to the cellar during the devastating air raids, he could only lie on his weary bed and hear the agonizing roar of explosions in the streets. The resourceful Germans had devised another secret weapon and from an incredible distance were bombarding Paris with their "Big Bertha." Two days after this new terror began, Emma Debussy knew that Claude could endure no more. At ten o'clock on the second night she could hear faintly a few broken words: "Come near, little one, come nearer to me!"

The grim requiem of the shells tolled on March 25, 1918, the night that Claude Debussy died. The beautiful farewell to his life's end is expressed in the words of René Peter, the most devoted of his friends.

"And it is ended. . . . There is left to me from this great friendship only a package of letters . . . and a small phonograph cylinder on which, a little while before the première of Pelléas, *I had recorded, sung by Debussy, the death of Mélisande. Alas, through having craved too often her harmonious secret, I have used up the precious wax. . . . The voice*

has worn itself out. Perhaps, once more, like a dying echo, it can still be heard . . . perhaps it is silent for ever. . . .

"A little of the living Debussy—is it there? I do not wish to know. Repose tranquilly in your wooden casket, dear treasure, who are so near to the void and yet who are eternal!"

Only seven months later came the Armistice. Had Debussy lived he would have seen the great arts of France arise reborn from her ashes. He would have watched the flowering of another generation of brilliant moderns to challenge his support and sympathy. And some of them would have looked to Claude Debussy for the leadership his achievements might have given them.

Untimely death at the age of fifty-six denied him a share in this reborn future of France. Nor did he live to realize that, after his lifelong struggle with doubt and dissension, the day was not far off when his name would be remembered forever, not only in French music, but in the music of the world.

APPENDICES

THE WORKS OF DEBUSSY

OPERA

1892-1902   Pelléas et Mélisande (Maurice Maeterlinck) Opera in five acts

ORCHESTRAL WORKS

1887   Printemps
1892-4   Prélude à l'après-midi d'un faune
1893-9   Nocturnes:
           Nuages
           Fêtes
           Sirènes (with female chorus)
1903-5   La Mer—Three symphonic sketches:
           De l'aube à midi sur la mer
           Jeux de vagues
           Dialogue du vent et de la mer
1904   Incidental music for *King Lear* (Shakespeare)
           Fanfare
           Sommeil de Lear
1906-12 Images:
-         Gigues
           Ibéria
           Rondes de printemps

WORKS FOR SOLO INSTRUMENT AND ORCHESTRA

1889   Fantaisie for piano and orchestra
1904   Danse sacrée and Danse profane for harp and strings

CHAMBER WORKS

1893   String Quartet
1903-5   Rhapsody for saxophone and piano

Chamber Works, *Continued:*

1909-10 Rhapsody for clarinet and piano
1910   Petite piece for clarinet and piano
1912   Syrinx for unaccompanied flute
1915   Sonata for 'cello and piano
         Sonata for flute, harp, and viola
1916-17 Sonata for piano and violin

PIANO WORKS

FOR PIANO DUET

1880   Symphonie en si (one movement)
1882 (?) Triomphe de Bacchus—Orchestral interlude
1889   Petite suite:
         1—En bateau
         2—Cortège
         3—Menuet
         4—Ballet
1891   Marche écossaise sur un thème populaire (The Earl of Ross
         March)
1914   Six èpigraphes antiques:
         Pour invoquer Pan, dieu de vent d'été
         Pour un tombeau sans nom
         Pour que la nuit soit propice
         Pour la danseuse aux crotales
         Pour l'égyptienne
         Pour remercier la pluie au matin

FOR TWO PIANOS

1901   Lindaraja
1915   En blanc et noir (Three pieces)

FOR SOLO PIANO

1880   Danse bohémienne
1888   Deux Arabesques
1890   Rêverie
         Ballade

Danse
Valse romantique
Nocturne
1890-1905 Suite Bergamasque:
    1—Prélude
    2—Menuet
    3—Clair de lune
    4—Passepied
1891 Mazurka
1896-1901 Pour le piano:
    1—Prélude
    2—Sarabande
    3—Toccata
1903 Estampes:
    1—Pagodes
    2—Soirée dans Grenade
    3—Jardins sous la pluie
1903 D'un cahier d'esquisses
1904 Masques
L'Ile joyeuse
1905 Images, Set I:
    1—Reflets dans l'eau
    2—Hommage à Rameau
    3—Mouvement
1907 Images, Set II:
    1—Cloches à travers les feuilles
    2—Et la lune descend sur le temple qui fut
    3—Poissons d'or
1906-8 Children's Corner Suite:
    1—Doctor Gradus ad Parnassum
    2—Jimbo's Lullaby
    3—Serenade for the Doll
    4—Snow is Dancing
    5—The Little Shepherd
    6—Golliwog's Cake-walk
1909 Hommage à Haydn

Piano Works, *Continued*:

1910   La plus que lente—Valse

1910   Préludes, Book I:

        1—Danseuses de Delphes

        2—Voiles

        3—Le Vent dans la plaine

        4—Les sons et les parfums tournent dans l'air du soir

        5—Les Collines d'Anacapri

        6—Des Pas sur la neige

        7—Ce qu'a vu le vent d'ouest

        8—La Fille aux cheveux de lin

        9—La Sérénade interrompue

        10—La Cathédrale engloutie

        11—La Danse de Puck

        12—Minstrels

1910-13   Préludes, Book II:

        1—Brouillards

        2—Feuilles mortes

        3—La Puerta del Vino

        4—Les Fées sont d'exquises danseuses

        5—Bruyères

        6—General Lavine—eccentric

        7—La Terrasse des audiences au clair de lune

        8—Ondine

        9—Hommage à S. Pickwick, Esq., P.P.M.P.C.

        10—Canope

        11—Les Tierces alternées

        12—Feux d'artifice

1913   La Boîte à joujoux—Children's ballet (scenario by André Hellé)

1914   Berceuse héroïque pour rendre hommage à S. M. le Roi Albert Ier de Belgique et à ses soldats

1915   12 Etudes:

       Book I:

        Pour les cinq doigts

        Pour les tierces

        Pour les quartes

        Pour les sixtes

Pour les octaves
Pour les huit doigts
Book II:
Pour les degrés chromatiques
Pour les agréments
Pour les notes répétées
Pour les sonorités opposées
Pour les arpèges
Pour les accords

CHORAL WORKS

1882   Printemps (Comte de Ségur)—Chorus for female voices

1883   Invocation (Lamartine)—Chorus for male voices (piano and vocal score only)

1884   L'Enfant prodigue (Édouard Guinand)—Cantata

1887-8   La Damoiselle élue (D. G. Rossetti—G. Sarrazin)—Cantata for solo voices, chorus, and orchestra

1908   Trois Chansons de Charles d'Orléans, for chorus unaccompanied:
Dieu! qu'il fait bon regarder!
Quand j'ai ouÿ le tabourin . . .
Yver, vous n'estes qu'un villain . . .

1911   Le Martyre de Saint Sébastien—Incidental music to the mystery play by Gabriele d'Annunzio, for solo voices, chorus, and orchestra

1912   Jeux—Ballet (scenario and choreography by Nijinsky)

1912   Khamma—Ballet (orchestrated by Charles Koechlin; scenario by W. L. Courtney and Maud Allan)

1916-17   Ode à la France (Louis Laloy)—Cantata for solo, chorus, and orchestra (completed by Marius-François Gaillard)

SONGS

1876 (?)   Nuit d'étoiles (Théodore de Banville)

1878 (?)   Beau soir (Paul Bourget)

Fleur des blés (André Girod)

[173]

1880-3   Mandoline (Paul Verlaine)
          La Belle au bois dormant (Vincent Hypsa)
          Voici que le printemps (Paul Bourget)
          Paysage sentimental (Paul Bourget)
1881   Zéphyr (Théodore de Banville)
1882 (1) Rondeau (Alfred de Musset)
1882 (4) Pantomime (Paul Verlaine)
          Clair de lune (Paul Verlaine)
          Pierrot (Théodore de Banville)
          Apparition (Stéphane Mallarmé)
1887-9   Cinq Poèmes de Baudelaire:
              1—Le Balcon
              2—Harmonie du soir
              3—Le Jet d'eau
              4—Recueillement
              5—La Mort des amants
1888   Ariettes oubliées (Paul Verlaine):
              1—C'est l'extase . . .
              2—Il pleure dans mon coeur . . .
              3—L'ombre des arbres . . .
              4—Chevaux de bois
              5—Green
              6—Spleen
1891   Deux Romances (Paul Bourget):
              1—Romance
              2—Les Cloches
          Les Angélus (G. le Roy)
          Dans le jardin (Paul Gravolet)
          Trois Mélodies (Paul Verlaine)
              1—La mer est plus belle . . .
              2—Le son du cor s'afflige . . .
              3—L'échelonnement des haies
1892   Fêtes galantes (Paul Verlaine), first series:
              1—En sourdine
              2—Fantoches
              3—Clair de lune

1892-3   Proses lyriques (Claude Debussy):
   1—De rêve
   2—De grève
   3—Des fleurs
   4—De soir

1897 Chansons de Bilitis (Pierre Louÿs):
   1—La Flûte de Pan
   2—La Chevelure
   3—Le Tombeau des Naïades

1904 Fêtes galantes (Paul Verlaine), second series:
   1—Les Ingénus
   2—Le Faune
   3—Colloque sentimental
  Trois Chansons de France:
   1—Rondel: Le temps a laissié son manteau . . . (Charles
    d'Orléans)
   2—La Grotte (Tristan L'Hermite)
   3—Rondel: Pour ce que plaisance est morte . . . (Charles
    d'Orléans)

1904-10   Le Promenoir des deux amants (Tristan L'Hermite):
   1—Auprès de cette grotte sombre . . .
   2—Crois mon conseil, chère Chimène . . .
   3—Je tremble en voyant ton visage . . .

1910 Trois Ballades de François Villon:
   1—Ballade de Villon à s'amye
   2—Ballade que feit Villon à la requeste de sa mère pour
    prier Nostre-Dame
   3—Ballade des femmes de Paris

1913 Trois Poèmes de Stéphane Mallarmé:
   1—Soupir
   2—Placet futile
   3—Éventail

1915 Noël des enfants qui n'ont plus de maisons (Claude Debussy)

ARRANGEMENTS AND ORCHESTRATIONS

GLUCK, C. W. Caprice for piano on airs from the ballet of *Alceste*

RAFF, J. Humoresque en forme de valse, arrangement for piano solo

SAINT-SAËNS, C. Arrangement for piano solo of extracts from the opera *Etienne Marcel*

Introduction et Rondo capriccioso, arrangement for two pianos

Second Symphony, arrangement for two pianos

SATIE, ERIK. Orchestration of Deux Gymnopédies

SCHUMANN, R. Am Springbrunnen, arrangement for two pianos

Six Studies in canon form, arrangement for two pianos

TCHAIKOVSKY, P. The Swan Lake, arrangement for three dances for piano solo

WAGNER, R. Overture to *The Flying Dutchman,* arrangement for two pianos

MAGAZINE ARTICLES *

Comoedia. November 4, 1909; January 31, December 17, 1910; January 26; May 18, 1911; February 1, 1914

Excelsior. March 9, 1911

Le Figaro. May 8, 1908; February 14, 1909

Gil Blas. January 12 to June 28, 1903

Mercure de France. January 1903

Musica. October 1902; May 1903; July 1906; January 1908; March 1911

La Revue blanche. April 1 to December 1, 1901

La Revue bleue. March and April 1904

La Revue S.I.M. November 1912 to May 15, 1913; November 1913 to March 1914

* A selection of these articles was made by Debussy in 1917 and entitled *Monsieur Croche antidilettante,* but it was not published until after his death.

RECORDINGS OF DEBUSSY'S WORKS

	RECORD NO.
(The) Afternoon of a Faun—*see* Prélude à l'après-midi d'un faune	
Arabesques Nos. 1 and 2, piano	
Jose Iturbi	V-18237
Walter Gieseking	C-17145D
Children's Corner Suite, piano	
Gieseking	in CM-314
A. Cortot	V-7147/8
Arr. for orch.—Paris Conservatory Orch., Coppola	VM-280
Arr. for flute, harp, and 'cello—Barrère, Salzedo, Britt	VM-639
No. 3 only, Sérénade à la poupée—Horowitz	V-1353
(*See also* Collections at the end)	
(La) Damoiselle élue—Soloists, St. Gervais Chorus, Pasdeloup Orch., Coppola	in VM-363
Danse (Tarantelle styrienne), piano	
Arr. for orchestra by Ravel—Boston Symphony Orch., Koussevitzky	V-7414
(2) Danses, harp and string orch.	
1. Danse sacrée. 2. Danse profane.	
E. Phillips, Phila. Orch., Stokowski	V-7455/6
(*See also* Collections at the end)	
En blanc et noir, two pianos	
Bartlett and Robertson	CX-241
L'Enfant prodigue, cantata	
Prélude, Cortège, and Air de danse—Opéra-Comique Orch., Gloëz	D-25417
Prelude, arr. for violin and piano—Heifetz and Sandor	V-1694
Recitative and Air de Lia	
D. Maynor, Phila. Orch., Ormandy	V-17698
Ninon Vallin	D-25848
Rose Bampton	V-7746
Recitative and Air d'Azaël—Charles Friant	D-25848

Recordings of Debussy's Works

Recordings of Debussy's Works

Recordings of Debussy's Works

No. 2, arr. for orch. by Ravel—Boston Symphony Orch.,
Koussevitzky — V-7375
No. 3—Percy Grainger — C-L1829
Prélude à l'après-midi d'un faune
London Philharmonic Orch., Beecham — C-69600D
Philadelphia Orch., Stokowski — V 6696
Arr. for piano—George Copeland — in VM-198
Preludes, piano, in two books (for titles *see* under Works,
p. 170)
Book I, 12 Preludes
Gieseking — CM-352
Cortot — VM-480
E. Robert Schmitz — VM-1031
No. 1, Dancers of Delphi—Paderewski — V-1521
No. 2, Voiles
Paderewski — V-1531
Copeland — V-14904
No. 4, Les sons et les parfums—E. Boynet — V-4419
No. 8, La Fille aux cheveux de lin
Arr. for violin and piano
Heifetz — V-6622
Kreisler — V-1358
Arr. for harp—Newell — C-700083D
No. 10, La Cathédrale engloutie
A. Rubinstein — V-36289
Gieseking — in CM-314
Copeland — in VM-198
Samaroff — V-7304
Arr. for orch.—Philadelphia Orch., Stokowski — in VM-116
Preludes, piano, Book II (for titles *see* under Works, page
170) *
Gieseking — CM-382
R. Casadesus — CM-644
No. 3, La Puerta del Vino—Copeland — V-14904

* The 12 Preludes of Book II are in some listings numbered as No. 1 to No. 12,
and in others as continuing the series begun in Book I—i.e., as No. 13 to No. 24.

RECORD NO.

No. 5, Bruyères
    Copeland   in VM-198
    Ania Dorfmann   C-DX803
No. 6, General Lavine, eccentric
    Copeland   in VM-198
    Ania Dorfmann   C-DX803
No. 7, La Terrasse des audiences—Copeland   in VM-198
No. 8, Ondine—Copeland   in VM-198
No. 10, Canope—Copeland   in VM-198
                 (*See also* Collections)
Printemps, symphonic suite—Paris Conservatory Orch.,
    Coppola   in VM-363
Quartet in G minor
    Budapest Quartet   CM-467
    Pro Arte Quartet   VM-186
Rêverie, piano—Gieseking   C-17138D
Rhapsody for clarinet and orchestra—Benny Goodman,
    N. Y. Philharmonic-Symphony Orch., Barbirolli   C-11517D
Rhapsody for saxophone and orchestra—Viard and Sym-
    phony Orch., Coppola   V-11426
Sonata No. 2 for flute, harp, and viola (or violin)
    Wummer, Newell, Katims   CX-282
    Moyse, Laskine, Merckel   VM-873
Sonata No. 3 for violin and piano
    Z. Francescatti and R. Casadesus   CMX-280
    Szigeti and Foldes   CX-242
    Elman and Mottman   VM-938

ALBUMS OF SONGS
(*not sold separately*)

Songs of Debussy—Maggie Teyte and Alfred Cortot
    Contains the following songs: VM-322
Auprès de cette grotte sombre (Le Promenoir des deux
    amants, No. 1)
Ballade des femmes de Paris

Recordings of Debussy's Works

Albums of Songs, *Continued:*

(La) Chevelure (Chansons de Bilitis, No. 2)

Clair de lune (Fêtes galantes, Set I, No. 3)

Colloque sentimental (Fêtes galantes, Set II, No. 3)

Crois mon conseil, chère Chimène (Promenoir des deux
    amants, No. 2)

De grève (Proses lyriques, No. 1)

En sourdine (Fêtes galantes, Set I, No. 1)

Fantoches (Fêtes galantes, Set I, No. 2)

(Le) Faune (Fêtes galantes, Set II, No. 2)

(La) Flûte de Pan (Chansons de Bilitis, No. 1)

(Les) Ingénus (Fêtes galantes, Set II, No. 1)

Je tremble en voyant ton visage (Promenoir des deux
    amants, No. 3)

(Le) Tombeau des Naïades (Chansons de Bilitis, No. 3)

Gramophone Shop Album—Maggie Teyte and Gerald
    Moore (no order number). Four songs:

De grève (Proses lyriques, No. 2)

Des fleurs (Cinq poèmes, No. 3)

De rêve (Proses lyriques, No. 1)

De soir (Proses lyriques, No. 4)

SEPARATE SONGS

Beau Soir—Claudia Muzio and orch.	C-4136M
Crois mon conseil, chère Chimène—Roger Bourdin	D-25945
Je tremble en voyant ton visage—Roger Bourdin	D-25945
Mandoline	
Lily Pons	V-1905
Roger Bourdin	D-25945
Voici que le printemps (Trois mélodies, No. 2) Povla Frijsh	V-18053
Aquarelles: Green (Ariettes oubliées, No. 5)	
Lily Pons	V-1905
Ninon Vallin	D-20326
(3) Chansons de Charles d'Orléans	
Nos. 1 and 3—Antwerp Cecilia Chorus and L. de Vocht	C-D19215

Recordings of Debussy's Works

Suite bergamasque, piano
  1. Prelude. 2. Menuet. 3. Clair de lune. 4. Passepied.
  No. 1, Prelude—M.-F. Gaillard   D-25021
  Nos. 1 and 2, Prelude and Menuet
    E. Robert Schmitz   V11-8694
    Gieseking   CMX-8
  No. 3, Clair de lune
    E. Robert Schmitz   V11-8240
    H. Bauer   V-7122
    Copeland   V-7963
  No. 3 arr. for orch.—Philadelphia Orchestra, Stokowski   V-1812

COLLECTIONS—ORCHESTRA

"Selected Works"—Philadelphia Orch., Stokowski   VM-116
  Nuages; La Cathédrale engloutie; Danses sacrée et profane

COLLECTIONS—PIANO

Album recorded by Gaby Casadesus   ASCH 103
  La Fille aux cheveux de lin (Preludes II, No. 8)
  Voiles (Preludes II, No. 2)
  Minstrels (Preludes II, No. 12)
  La Sérénade interrompue (Preludes II, No. 9)
  Golliwog's Cake-walk (Children's Corner)
  Sérénade à la poupée (Children's Corner)
  Two Arabesques
Album recorded by George Copeland   VM-198
  Preludes Nos. 10, 17, 18, 19, 20, 22 (La Cathédrale en-
    gloutie; Bruyères; General Lavine; La Terrasse
    des audiences; Ondine; Canope)
  Prélude à l'après-midi d'un faune (arr. by Copeland)
  Soirée dans Grenade (Estampes, No. 2)
  Clair de lune (Suite bergamasque, No. 3)
Album recorded by Walter Gieseking   CM-314
  Children's Corner Suite

Collections—Piano, *Continued:*
Suite bergamasque
La Cathédrale engloutie (Preludes I, No. 10)
Reflets dans l'eau (Images, I, No. 1)
Soirée dans Grenade (Estampes, No. 2)
Album recorded by Artur Rubinstein   VM-998
Soirée dans Grenade (Estampes, No. 2)
Jardins sous la pluie (Estampes, No. 3)
Reflets dans l'eau (Images, Set I, No. 1)
Hommage à Rameau (Images, Set I, No. 2)
La Plus que lente, Valse

ARRANGED BY DEBUSSY

Satie's Gymnopédie—Boston Symphony Orchestra, Koussevitzky   V-7252

GENERAL INDEX

General Index

INDEX OF DEBUSSY'S WORKS
MENTIONED IN THE TEXT

Index of Works